NEW AND EXPANDED EDITION

REAL PRESENCE

The Work of Eucharist

NATHAN MITCHELL

LTP

LITURGY
TRAINING
PUBLICATIONS

Acknowledgments

The author is grateful to Cyril Gorman, OSB, doctoral student in theology and graduate assistant at the Notre Dame Center for Pastoral Liturgy. With a critical eye and painstaking attention to detail, he brought the text from manuscript to final copy.

The scripture quotations contained herein are from the *New Revised Standard Version of the Bible: Catholic Edition*, © 1993, 1998 by the Division of Christian Education of the National Council of Churches of Christ in the U.S.A. Used by permission, all rights reserved.

Excerpts from the English translation of the *Catechism of the Catholic Church* for use in the United States of America, © 1994 United States Catholic Conference—Libreria Editrice Vaticana. All rights reserved.

The first, second and fourth essays in their entirety and part of the third essay appeared originally in *Liturgy Digest* 4:2 (1998), © 1998 Notre Dame Center for Pastoral Liturgy.

The cover image is from The Pierpont Morgan Library/Art Resource, New York City: S0037918, M.44,F.7, color transparency: "Christ washing the feet of the Apostles," manuscript page, France, twelfth or thirteenth century. The background image is by PhotoDisc, Inc.

Printed in the United States of America.

16 15 14 13 12   2 3 4 5 6

Library of Congress Cataloging-in-Publication Data
Mitchell, Nathan.
    Real Presence : the work of Eucharist / Nathan Mitchell.—
New and expanded ed.
       p.   cm.
Includes bibliographical references.
    ISBN 1-56854-407-3
    1. Lord's Supper—Catholic Church. 2. Catholic
Church—Liturgy. I. Title.
    BX2215.2 .M57 2001
    234'.163DC21

2001029786

RLPR

Contents

Introduction

When the first edition of this book appeared in 1998, Christians were eagerly awaiting the advent of the third millennium. Despite ominous forecasts of cataclysm and chaos, the year 2000 arrived with relatively few disruptions to daily life. Meanwhile, many of the pre-2000 debates—about the ongoing renewal of liturgy, about the eucharist as a sacrament central to Catholic identity, about how to build or renovate spaces for public worship, about "Sunday celebrations in the absence of a priest"—have continued into the twenty-first century. They are not likely to disappear any time soon.

It has been said, quite rightly, that controversies about the liturgy are always about more than the liturgy. They are about deeply held convictions touching the relationship between church and culture, the nature of Catholic community (inclusive or exclusive), the prospects for faith in a "culture of disbelief." In his 1997 book *The Future of Eucharist,* Professor Bernard Cooke addresses the question "What is distinctly Catholic?" "Catholics come to eucharist," he writes, "quite satisfied with being 'American' and no longer see their parish as a refuge from cultural alienation" (Cooke 1997, 36). Cooke goes on to observe that in the United States today, Catholics are far more ecumenical in their outlook than they were a generation or two ago. They see other Christians as partners in the journey of faith. Indeed, one of the great benefits of post-conciliar liturgical renewal has been the emergence of a common lectionary system. Though not used by all, this common lectionary guarantees that large numbers of Christian congregations in this country proclaim, preach and study the same scriptures Sunday by Sunday. Has this emerging ecumenism eroded traditional Catholic beliefs about eucharist? Not at all, says Bernard Cooke; it simply shows that eucharist, for many Catholics, is no longer "an assertion of ethnic culture" but a treasure shared in common with other Christians.

Still, there are those who feel that "Americanization" represents a loss, a serious threat to the distinctive identity of Roman Catholics on this continent. Perhaps the classic formulation of this anxiety appeared in an essay by the late Mark Searle. Summarizing the results of a study of American Catholic life in English-speaking parishes during the mid-1980s, Searle wrote:

> [T]here is strong evidence that American Catholics are in the process of becoming more characteristically American than characteristically Catholic. In other words, cultural assimilation appears to be occurring at the expense of a distinctive Catholic identity. In their moral, political and social attitudes, Catholics are becoming indistinguishable from the rest of the population. Where liturgy is concerned, this means a growing alienation from precisely that sense of collective identity and collective responsibility which the liturgy might be thought to rehearse. It is a threat to the integrity of the liturgical act. Far from being able to inure Catholics against the negative aspects of their wider culture, the liturgy may actually be succumbing to such influences. (Searle 1986, 333)

This debate continues today. Most Roman Catholics would probably identify themselves as belonging to a "eucharistic church," a community whose principal Sunday celebration has been for many centuries—and still is—the celebration of Mass. But some point to the phenomenon of "Sunday celebrations in the absence of a priest" as a sign that Catholic eucharistic identity is seriously at risk. Thus, James Dallen writes in *The Dilemma of Priestless Sundays*:

Introduction

To deny the eucharist to a community is to deny it full ecclesial-
ity. Both denials are implied in the inability or refusal to provide
a community with an ordained pastoral leader. To do so is a
threat to ministry, both ordained and lay. It is also a threat to
the local community. And it is a threat to the church and to the
identity and mission of Catholic Christianity, which rest solidly
upon sacramental foundations. (Dallen 1994, 127)

Bernard Cooke is more optimistic. The fact that "fewer parishes
have their own resident eucharistic leader" does not necessarily mean
"decline" (Cooke 1997, 1–2). It may also lead to a improvement—of
both eucharist and the community celebrating it. As Cooke notes,
"Catholics are increasingly aware that they along with the ordained
presider are the *doers* of the liturgical action. . . . Laywomen and men
are in many places taking roles intrinsic to the liturgical action"
(3–4). In short, what is happening is a transformation of church life
itself, one aspect of which is "an invasion of the sacred by 'unconse-
crated' laity that touches implicitly the whole power-base of the
ordained clergy" (5). To some, this "invasion" represents an obstacle;
to others, it represents opportunity.

This revised and expanded edition of *Real Presence: The Work
of Eucharist* examines some of the factors that are currently shaping
discussions of eucharist, especially among Roman Catholics. Biblical
scholarship, recent theological research and cultural studies (for
example, the work of George Steiner, discussed in the fourth essay)
are highlighted. An addition to the third essay (on Luke as a
"eucharistic" gospel), as well as an entirely new fifth essay (on
eucharist in the work of some contemporary European theologians),
have been included in this revised and expanded edition. The first
edition's "Resources" section—now somewhat outdated—has been
replaced with a list of pastoral resources available from Liturgy
Training Publications. Readers are also encouraged to look for
updated bibliographies on eucharist specifically (and liturgy in general) online (see, for example, the website of the Notre Dame Center
for Pastoral Liturgy: www.nd.edu/~ndcpl).

Special thanks to Gabe Huck and the staff of Liturgy Training
Publications in Chicago for their continued interest in this work.

—*Nathan Mitchell*

References to Works Cited in the Text

Cooke, Bernard. 1997. *The Future of Eucharist*. New York: Paulist Press.

Dallen, James. 1994. *The Dilemma of Priestless Sundays*. Chicago: Liturgy Training Publications.

Searle, Mark. 1986. "The Notre Dame Study of Catholic Parish Life." *Worship* 60:312–33.

Catholics and Eucharist: Preliminary Issues

Catholic Identity under Siege?

In 1994, the *New York Times* carried two reports on American religion that aroused particular interest among Roman Catholics. One was an essay entitled "Future of Faith Worries Catholic Leaders" by Peter Steinfels. Steinfels's essay formed the conclusion of a series entitled "Searching Its Soul: The American Catholic Church." The article began by inviting readers to contrast two images: The first was the awesome scene of 400,000 teenagers in a Rocky Mountain park in the summer of 1993. They were there to celebrate World Youth Day, joining Pope John Paul II in a festival of prayer and praise. The second image arose from the prolonged anxiety, agitation and anger that had been building as a result of resignations by highly placed prelates, widespread reports of sexual misconduct on the part of the clergy, and by the papal reaffirmation (in *Ordinatio sacerdotalis*) that the priesthood is restricted to males and that the matter is no longer open to debate among faithful Catholics. Steinfels wrote:

> No one imagines that American Catholicism . . . will soon disappear. But church leaders increasingly wonder whether the church, even as its ranks increase and it draws new energy from the latest waves of immigrants, is losing its distinctive identity. . . .

[T]he strong feelings stirred by issues [like contraception, abortion, divorce, sexual morality] may be hampering the church's response to a less visible but more pervasive problem, what worried leaders inside the church have begun calling a "hollowing out" or "thinning" of Catholicism.

Echoing the 1983 "Nation at Risk" federal report on the decline of public education in the United States, Marcel J. Dumestre, director of the Institute for Ministry at Loyola University in New Orleans, says, "We are a church at risk." (Steinfels 1994, 1[A])

Steinfels illustrated these three concerns—that the church is losing its "distinctive identity"; that its traditional doctrines and ethics have been irretrievably eroded, "hollowed out" or "thinned"; and that the church itself is "at risk"—by citing the results of an April 1994, *New York Times*/CBS News poll that indicated that "almost two-thirds of American Catholics believe that during Mass . . . the bread and wine can best be understood as 'symbolic reminders of Christ' rather than as actually being changed into Christ's body and blood. Even among the subgroup of Catholics who said they attended Mass every week or almost every week, 51 percent described the rite as *strictly symbolic*" (12[A], emphasis added).

Of course, as Steinfels noted, a complex religious belief burdened with a long and sometimes bitterly disputed theological pedigree cannot be adequately measured by a polling process. Still, considering the centrality of eucharistic faith and praxis to Catholic identity over two millennia, it is perhaps astonishing that so many respondents seemed to doubt that in the sacramental species Christ "whole and entire, body and blood, soul and divinity" is really, truly and substantially present under the appearances of bread and wine. This formula has been central to the sacramental teaching of the Roman church for more than 400 years. The words used in the decree *De sanctissima eucharistia* during the second period of the Council of Trent (under Pope Julius III) were these:

> *Principio docet sancta Synodus et aperte ac simpliciter profitetur, in almo sanctae Eucharistiae sacramento post panis et vini consecrationem Dominum nostrum Iesus Christum verum Deum atque hominem vere, realiter ac substantialiter sub specie*

illarum rerum sensibilium contineri. [First, the holy synod teaches—and openly and simply declares—that after the consecration of bread and wine, our Lord Jesus Christ, true God and true man, is truly, really and substantially contained under the appearance of those sensible elements.] (Denzinger-Schönmetzer, *Enchiridion symbolorum,* 1636)

[S]tatim post consecrationem verum Domini nostri corpus verumque eius sanguinem sub panis et vini specie una cum ipsius anima et divinitate exsistere. [Immediately after the consecration, the true body of the Lord—and his true blood—exist under the appearance of bread and wine, together with his soul and divinity.] (#1640)

Totus enim et integer Christus sub panis specie et sub quavis ipsius speciei parte, totus item sub vini specie et sub eius partibus exsistit. [For whole and entire Christ exists under the species of bread (and under each part of that species); similarly, he exists under the species of wine (and under each part of that species).] (#1641)

These familiar texts would seem to make the Roman Catholic church's position on eucharistic real presence unmistakably clear. Yet the statistics cited in Steinfels's essay seem to suggest that allegiance to the doctrine of real presence, at least among American Catholics, has eroded. In short, the Roman church's eucharistic teaching may be facing a "thinning" or "hollowing out," and this could have potentially devastating long-term effects on Catholic identity.

Similar conclusions had been reached in the mid-1980s in a five-year research study conducted by Notre Dame's Institute for Pastoral and Social Ministry (now known as the Institute for Church Life) and funded by the Lilly Endowment. Overall, the study found that Catholic parishes had embraced the liturgical reforms of Vatican II emphatically, if not always exuberantly. In less than a generation's time, the celebration of eucharist among American Roman Catholics had undergone a complete transformation. Latin had disappeared; a new lectionary was in place and universally in use; a homily could be heard at virtually every Sunday Mass; the new *Ordo missae* was "observed more or less intact"; and the overwhelming majority of participants go to communion" (Searle 1986, 316).

As the 1985 extraordinary synod of bishops observed, "the liturgical renewal is the most visible fruit of the whole conciliar effort." This conclusion was amply supported by the data gathered in the Notre Dame study. However, that study also revealed some trends that were gaining momentum a decade later—trends of the sort Steinfels discussed in his *New York Times* essay.

Summarizing the study's findings on liturgical reform and renewal in predominantly Caucasian, English-speaking parishes, for example, Mark Searle drew attention to a number of disquieting conclusions. First, Searle noted, most people seem to consider the eucharist *more a 'source' than a 'summit'* . . . more a matter of sustenance than a thing of ecstasy." Less than half the people surveyed mentioned "Sunday Mass" as their most satisfying religious activity (331).

Second, a rather significant percentage of regular, Mass-going Catholics expressed *indifference about the rites, texts and symbols of the liturgy;* about the role of the assembly, of music and song, of word and gesture; or about the relation between worship and the responsibilities of Christian life, collective or personal. Their attitude seemed passive rather than engaged: "just tell us what to do and we'll do it" (331).

Third, Searle and his colleagues found a *very fluid sense of ecclesial boundaries,* a "confused sense of the difference between belonging and not belonging to the church." For example, Searle noted, "a traditional way of discriminating between practicing and lapsed Catholics was whether they went to Mass, but 53 percent of suburban Catholics thought that never going to Mass did not put a person outside the church." In short, many Americans seem to espouse a "pragmatic ecclesiology of voluntary association" rather than a disciplined, boundary-conscious ecclesiology based on creed, cult, ethics and action (332).

Finally, Searle and his colleagues discovered that *rugged American individualism had impacted not only the social fabric but religious identity as well.* In this, Searle's conclusions were similar to those reached by Robert Bellah and his associates in their well-known book *Habits of the Heart.* Bellah noted that for most

Americans, individualism (defined as making self-interest the criterion for determining what is good, true, valuable and moral) has eclipsed communal structures and meanings. Traditionally, for instance, churches have thought of themselves as "communities of worship." Worship is the context within which believers enact their relation to God, others and world. Worship embodies memories in story, rehearses ethical and social obligations, and articulates hopes for the future. In traditional religion, public worship "establishes patterns of character and virtue that should operate in economic and political life" (Bellah 1985, 227). This traditional pattern

> assumes a certain priority of the religious community over the individual. The community exists before the individual is born and will continue after his or her death. The relationship of the individual to God . . . is mediated by the whole pattern of community life. There is a givenness about the community and the tradition. They are not normally a matter of individual choice." (227)

In his summary of the results of the Notre Dame study, Searle highlighted Bellah's conclusions by noting that

> there is strong evidence that American Catholics are in the process of becoming more characteristically American than characteristically Catholic. In other words, cultural assimilation appears to be occurring at the expense of a distinctive Catholic identity. In their moral, political and social attitudes, Catholics are becoming indistinguishable from the rest of the population. Where liturgy is concerned, this means a growing alienation from precisely that sense of collective identity and collective responsibility which the liturgy might be thought to rehearse. It is a threat to the integrity of the liturgical act. Far from being able to inure Catholics against the negative aspects of their wider culture, the liturgy may actually be succumbing to such influences. (Searle 1986, 333)

If what Bellah, Searle and Steinfels report is true, there is good reason to believe (1) that cultural assimilation is replacing Catholic identity; (2) that personal values of self-interest are replacing the communal virtues proposed by the liturgy as the basis for moral, political and social activity; and (3) that the eucharist is rapidly becoming what retired Yale University professor Aidan Kavanagh once called a celebration of the middle-class values of consumerism, participation in approved groups and comfort in affluence—politically correct values of joining, meeting, speaking out, affirming individual distinctiveness and creating community as *feeling* rather than form (Kavanagh 1990, 102). The eucharistic liturgy, Kavanagh complained, is increasingly seen as an opportunity to "ministerialize" the middle-class laity, to *move away from* the arts of ceremony and symbol toward "verbalization as the assembly's main medium of communication within itself." The result, he says, is a "bourgeoisie-ifying" of the church's worship:

> Iconography is disappearing in our new church buildings, giving way to potted plants and shopping-mall-like spaces. These tendencies obscure a sense of sacramentality and of the divine presence as something distinct from and transcending the community at worship. When one adds to this the understandable if often aggressive and ill-considered attempts unilaterally to alter liturgical language and the ways it names God . . . the liturgy becomes perceived by many as less an obedient standing in the alarming presence of the living God in Christ than a tiresome dialectical effort at raising the consciousness of middle-class groups concerning ideologically approved ends and means. (102)

Another View

For scholars like Bellah, Searle and Kavanagh, the past is truly prologue. What has gripped our national life for decades is now co-opting ecclesial life. Just as individualism has subverted our social and political institutions (leaving us with gridlocked governments, insurance that does not insure, murder as a celebrity event and cities controlled by crime), so now it threatens to destroy traditional religious identity.

A rather different view of the situation has been put forward by priest-sociologist Andrew Greeley. In an essay entitled "Because of the Stories," Greeley argues that any "erosion" of Catholic identity results not from a failure on the part of lay people to adhere to traditional doctrine, but from the authoritarianism and ineffectiveness of the church's leadership. Today, Greeley observes, the church comes across as

> resolutely authoritarian . . . proud of the fact that "it is not a democracy." It discriminates against women and homosexuals. It tries to regulate the bedroom behavior of married men and women. It tries to impose the Catholic position regarding abortion on everyone. It represses dissent and disagreement. The Vatican seems obsessed with sex. The Pope preaches against birth control in countries with rapidly expanding populations. . . . Bishops and priests are authoritarian and insensitive. Lay people have no control of how their contributions are spent. . . . The church has covered up sexual abuse by priests for decades. Now it is paying millions of dollars to do penance for the sexual amusements of supposedly celibate priests while it seeks to minimize, if not eliminate altogether, the sexual pleasures of married lay people. (Greeley 1994, 38)

In spite of such failures, however, Greeley argues that Catholics do not seem to be leaving the church in droves. On the contrary, the actual rate of defection from the church remains today what it was in 1960, roughly 15 percent. Indeed, as the overall population of the United States has increased since the 1960s, the Catholic population has kept pace. Greeley suggests that this phenomenon of relatively steady church membership and participation results from the rather simple fact that Catholics like being Catholic. Such lay people, he concluded, refuse to be driven from the church by their leaders' unawareness of or insensitivity to their lives. Their faith is nurtured by stories and images, by customs and devotions that have a stronger hold on the religious imagination than decrees or doctrines.

All this, it may be suggested, has a profound impact on understanding the eucharist as a primary source of Catholic identity. Since the Second Vatican Council, lay people have claimed ownership of the eucharistic celebration in ways perhaps unique in the church's history. Whether or not such ownership represents what Aidan Kavanagh has called "a ministerialization of the middle-class laity" is open to debate, but the fact remains that "full, conscious and active participation" has caught hold, even when (as the Notre Dame Study of Catholic Parish Life found) the style of celebration often seems mechanical and listless, and the quality of music and preaching is poor (Searle 1986, 319). The fact remains that a majority of Roman Catholics still find in the eucharist their primary resource for understanding God, church and world; for meeting life's goals and destiny; for reviewing and renewing meanings, values and relationships. In short, the eucharist remains the premier ritual occasion through which people negotiate their connections with God and community.

Catholic identity is thus shaped primarily by art and image, word and rite, story and ceremony. Professor Lee Kirkpatrick of the College of William and Mary suggests that one important reason for Catholicism's endurance and vigor as a religious heritage lies in the fact that it offers "so many objects of potential attachment" (Greeley 1994, 41). In other words, Catholic tradition provides numerous ritual and devotional "entry points." The points are, in the main, doxological rather than doctrinal in character and content. As Aidan Kavanagh writes in his study *The Shape of Baptism,* Christian identity begins not in a classroom but "in the soil, in the barnyard, in the slaughterhouse; amid the quiet violence of the garden, strangled cries, and fat spitting in the pan. . . . [They] depend on something's having been grabbed by the throat" (Kavanagh 1978, 160). He concludes that the "classroom" within which Christians learn their true identity is

> a river, pool, bath house, or tomb. Their language is asceticism, good works, exorcism, bathing and anointing and dining. Their purpose is gradually to ease one into the love of God for the world through Jesus Christ in his life-giving Spirit, and to do so after the manner in which the Son . . . consummated the same divine mystery by death and resurrection. . . . The Christian stands deep in all this, naked, covered with nothing but water and oil as night turns into day and as the fast becomes the Mother of Feasts. This is more than just a saving from sin or a classroom syllabus: it is . . . the divinization of humankind concretely accomplished through the incarnate [One] dying and rising still among [the] faithful. (158–59)

As the *Catechism of the Catholic Church* (CCC) notes, eucharist is the climax of precisely those mysteries of initiation through which Christian identity is acquired, enacted and celebrated (#1322). In sum, Catholic identity is not syllabus but sacrament. Thus, while rugged American individualism may well constitute a serious challenge to social and ecclesial life, it is not yet clear whether Catholics have simply "succumbed" to cultural assimilation or whether they have become "more characteristically American than characteristically Catholic." As Parker J. Palmer has observed, it would be a serious mistake for church leaders to pit "faith" against "culture" in a society as diverse, complex and pluralistic as ours. Terms like "community" and "individualism," "public sector" and "private," need not cancel each other:

> [I]n a healthy society the private and the public are not mutually exclusive, not in competition with each other. They are, instead, two halves of a whole, two poles of a paradox. They work together dialectically, helping to create and nurture one another. . . .
>
> Perhaps the most important ministry the church can have in the renewal of public life is a "ministry of paradox": not to resist the inward turn of American spirituality on behalf of effective public action, *but to deepen and direct and discipline that inwardness in the light of faith* until God leads us back to a vision of the public and to faithful action on the public's behalf. (Palmer 1983, 31, 155)

Among Roman Catholics, eucharist is perhaps the arena where this deepening, directing and disciplining of "inwardness" takes place—the arena where the impulse to withdraw into a purely private spirituality is constantly "corrected" and "refocused" through the biblical impulse to see religion as involved with the whole of life. (See Bellah 1985, 248.) The eucharist, in other words, is the place where Catholics regularly rediscover that (as Andrew Greeley says) "religion is experience, image, story and poem before it is anything else." Robert Bellah himself recognized this crucial point in an essay published nearly 30 years ago:

Guard the real presence! Do not let the Eucharist sink into [mere] memory and commemoration. . . . I do not mean guard *theories* about the real presence . . . for the real presence is not a theory—it is an experienced, present spiritual reality. That is its power for us. . . .

[F]or too long the disembodied intellect, Protestant literalism or Catholic rationalism, has tyrannized over experience. Theology is a servant of a totally embodied religious experience and religious vision; it is not its master. The great symbols of the Eucharist cannot be finally captured in any theology.

At the moment we need not so much an overall abstract explanation as to hear what the symbols [themselves]—the bread and the wine, the fraction and the communion, the stone and the water—are saying. *We need to let them speak and we need to listen.* In our technological age we have been too concerned with the technique of liturgy, with its manipulation, rather than with listening and contemplation.

The Eucharist can, if we let it, speak to our condition, as the Quakers used to say, with peculiar appropriateness, for it makes no assertion except out of negation and it sees no wholeness except out of annihilation. It is the supreme ritual expression of brokenness and death, of homelessness and landlessness. It consecrates all the good things of the earth and it promises renewal and rebirth not only for the individual but for society and the cosmos. And yet it makes us restless on this earth: it makes us see the conditional, and provisional, and broken quality of all things human. (Bellah 1973, 232–34)

By claiming ownership of the postconciliar liturgy, Roman Catholics may well be reclaiming their distinctive identity as *sacramentum mundi,* as sacrament of God's plan for the universe, a plan celebrated and renewed in the eucharist. They have not done this at the level of rigorous intellectual exactitude but at precisely the level of poem and metaphor, symbol and story, art and ritual.

A degree of inarticulateness about doctrinal precision (such as that which surfaced in the *New York Times*/CBS News poll mentioned above) may not be cause for alarm. Over the centuries, Catholic lay people have often regarded the professional theologians' rigorous "major and minor premises," "middle terms" and "square of oppositions" with bemused skepticism. Average medieval Catholics, for example, may have had a deep faith in the real presence, even though they probably could not have explained why a Roman council in the year 1059 forced Berengarius of Tours to swear that "the bread and wine placed on the altar after the consecration are not only a sacrament but the true body and blood of our Lord Jesus Christ . . . physically *[sensualiter]* and truly *[in veritate]* touched and broken by the hands of the priest and torn by the teeth of the faithful" (Denzinger-Schönmetzer, 690). Nor could the average medieval Catholic two centuries later have told you why Thomas Aquinas rejected the obvious and literal sense of the Berengarian confession and instead argued that

> [T]he body of Christ is not eaten as under its natural form, but as under the sacramental species. For this reason, St. Augustine, commenting on John 6.63 ("The spirit gives life, the flesh is of no avail"), said: "This verse is directed against those who understand Christ carnally. For there are some who think that the [eucharistic] body of Christ is like flesh torn in strips from a corpse or sold in a butcher shop." [On the contrary, Aquinas continues], *the body of Christ in itself is not broken, but only in its sacramental appearance.* And this is the sense in which we should understand Berengarius's profession of faith; *the fraction and the chewing with the teeth refer to the sacramental species,* underneath which the body of Christ is really present. (*Summa Theologiae,* IIIa.77.7, *ad tertium,* emphasis added)

The point, of course, is that throughout history, most Catholics have expressed their eucharistic faith in ritual and symbol, not in propositions. Their belief in real presence was expressed in narrative and devotion, in image and art. Medieval believers, who could not have told you the difference between Berengarius and Beelzebub, might have had no qualms at all burying the eucharistic species in their gardens to insure the fertility of their crops. To modern believers, this sounds like the worst of misguided medieval magic, gross sacrilege and rank heresy. But at another level—the dense, multivalent level of symbolic action—the deed is not as superstitious or debased as it seems. While no one today would want to imitate the medieval gardener's action, there is a certain degree of symbolic sense to it. To lay the Lord's body in the earth is to affirm that through the mystery of the incarnate Word the world itself has somehow become "God's body," and that in the flesh of the Risen One the awaited transfiguration of *all* matter has begun. As theologian Karl Rahner once wrote in a homily for the feast of the Ascension,

> We Christians are the most sublime of materialists. . . . We recognize and believe that matter will last forever and be glorified forever. . . . [We believe that this world] is already filled with the forces of this indescribable transformation, this inner dynamism which Paul, speaking of the resurrection of the flesh, called the Holy Breath of God. We believe that this Spirit of God, this power of all powers, this meaning of all meanings, is now present at the very heart and center of *all* reality, including material reality, and has already, in the glorified flesh of Christ, brought the beginning of the world triumphantly to its . . . perfection. The universal and glorious transfiguration of the world . . . has already begun. (Rahner 1977, 183–84)

The medieval gardeners may have failed in matters of nuanced theological speculation, but they were geniuses in matters of symbol, story, image and ritual. They intuitively understood what Robert Bellah alluded to in his essay on "Liturgy and Experience":

> Theology is a servant of a totally embodied religious experience and religious vision; it is not its master. The great symbols of the Eucharist cannot be finally captured in any theology. Their inexhaustible depth of meaning can be explained in different and even contradictory ways by a variety of theologies without their own inward vitality being affected. . . .
>
> [W]e need . . . to hear what the symbols . . . are saying. We need to let *them* speak and we need to listen. (Bellah 1973, 233)

References to Works Cited in the Text

Bellah, Robert. 1973. "Liturgy and Experience." In *The Roots of Ritual,* edited by James Shaugnessy. Grand Rapids: Eerdmans.

———. 1985. *Habits of the Heart.* Berkeley: University of California Press.

Greeley, Andrew. 1994. "Because of the Stories." *New York Times Sunday Magazine,* 10 July 1994.

Kavanagh, Aidan. 1978. *The Shape of Baptism.* Collegeville: The Liturgical Press/Pueblo.

———. 1990. "Liturgical Inculturation: Looking to the Future." *Studia Liturgica* 20:95–106.

Palmer, Parker J. 1983. *The Company of Strangers: Christians and the Renewal of America's Public Life.* New York: Crossroad.

Rahner, Karl. 1977. "The Festival of the Future of the World." In *Theological Investigations,* vol. 7. Translated by David Bourke. New York: Seabury.

Searle, Mark. 1986. "The Notre Dame Study of Catholic Parish Life." *Worship* 60:312–33.

Steinfels, Peter. 1994. "Future of Faith Worries Catholic Leaders." *New York Times,* 1 June 1994.

Thomas Aquinas. 1963. *Summa Theologiae,* vol. 58. Translated by William Barden. New York: McGraw-Hill.

Eucharist in the *Catechism* of the *Catholic Church*

S ome commentators on church matters have assumed that the publication of the *Catechism of the Catholic Church* (CCC) was aimed at stopping doctrinal erosion—or "hollowing out"—by reasserting traditional Catholic teaching. As the pages that follow will show, however, the catechism may move in that direction, but it also opens up fresh perspectives, especially in the area of eucharistic faith and practice. This chapter will thus be divided into two sections: (1) preliminary observations about the nature of the catechism itself; and (2) a sketch of its eucharistic teaching.

Preliminary Observations

A Work in Progress

Perhaps the most useful way to think about the *Catechism of the Catholic Church* is to regard it as a work in progress. It does not claim to be an exhaustive account of all Catholic doctrines; it is rather an invitation to critical reflection—to a sustained, collaborative

6dialogue—about the principal foundations and formulas of Roman Catholic faith and praxis. The catechism's publication marks the beginning of a process, not a conclusion. A magnificent disclaimer early in the book bears this out:

> By design, this Catechism does not set out to provide the adaptation of doctrinal presentations and catechetical methods required by the differences of culture, age, spiritual maturity, and social and ecclesial condition among all those to whom it is addressed. Such indispensable adaptations are the responsibility of particular catechisms and, even more, of those who instruct the faithful. (#24)

Clearly, the new catechism was not intended to be used simply "as is." Just as the Constitution on the Sacred Liturgy *Sacrosanctum concilium* (SC) has made inculturation an essential principle of liturgical renewal (#37–40)—thereby establishing a mandate broader and deeper than the simple creation of a new liturgical "library"—so the catechism has applied the same principle to Christian catechesis and mystagogy with equal vigor. In this, the catechism is not only reaffirming the pastoral strategy of Vatican II, it is also reasserting the position of the old *Catechismus romanus* (CR)—the "Catechism of the Council of Trent"—which warns that *Christian formation and catechesis must be adapted to the varying aptitudes and customs of peoples and cultures.* Its preface insists that "[t]he age, the natural abilities, the cultural customs and the particular circumstances of those to be catechized must be considered" (*Observanda est enim audientium aetas, ingenium, mores, conditio, ut qui docendi munus exercet omnia omnibus efficiatur, ut et omnes Christo lucrifaciat";* Rodríguez 1989, Preface 11). Teachers were admonished *against* the illusion that all people can or should be taught "by one and the same method or formula" *(Neque vero unius tantum generis homines fidei suae commissos esse arbitretur, ut praescripta quadam et certa docendi formula erudire atque ad veram pietatem instituere aeque omnes fideles possit).*

Catechism and Culture

Thus, the greatest and most far-reaching contribution of the *Catechism of the Catholic Church* may lie not in what it says but in what it does not say. It provides for reimaging faith, for reshaping catechesis according to the indigenous, God-given resources of *particular* peoples in *local* cultures. Fidelity to the mandate found in article 24 of the catechism consists not in repeating its formulas but in adapting its contents to the conditions of the cultures in which Christians find themselves. It is for precisely this reason that Paul VI spoke of "the unceasing interplay" between "the gospel and [humanity's] actual [life], both personal and social" (*Evangelii nuntiandi*, 29). The fundamental purpose of catechesis is not to defend doctrine, but to proclaim the gospel. Indeed, the church exists in order to evangelize, and the always begins "by being evangelized itself":

> The church . . . is the community of hope lived and communicated, the community of mutual love; and it needs to listen unceasingly to what it must believe, to its reasons for hoping, to the new commandment of love. It is the People of God immersed in the world, often tempted by idols, and it always needs to hear the proclamation of those "mighty works of God" which first converted it to the Lord; it always needs to be called together afresh . . . and reunited. (*Evangelii nuntiandi*, 15, author's translation)

As multicultural evangelizer and catechist, the church is simultaneously teacher *and* pupil, the one who speaks and instructs, and the one who listens and learns. Thus, the 1994 document "Fourth Instruction for the Right Application of the Conciliar Constitution on the Liturgy," released by the Congregation for Divine Worship and the Discipline of the Sacraments in April 1994, spoke of inculturation as a two-way street, a "double movement" through which the gospel penetrates "a given socio-cultural milieu," while at the same time the church assimilates those authentic cultural values that can deepen the understanding of Christ's message and enrich liturgical celebration.

The *Catechism of the Catholic Church* thus stands squarely in the tradition of the sixteenth-century *Catechismus romanus,* which fundamentally redefined the nature and purpose of a catechism. No longer is such a document to be regarded as a medieval *malleus maleficarum vel haereticorum,* a hammer to be used against witches or heretics. No longer is it to be viewed as an arsenal of unassailable arguments aimed at settling all doctrinal debates. Rather, catechisms are to be understood as supple tools that invite and welcome adaptation in order to extend and enrich the ongoing conversation between church and cultures, between catechists and individuals. Such adaptations, the catechism asserts, are not optional; they are "indispensable," for the ultimate pastoral principle that must guide all catechisms is "the love that never ends":

> The whole concern of doctrine and its teaching must be directed to the love that never ends. Whether something is proposed for belief, for hope or for action, the love of our Lord must always be made accessible, so that anyone can see that all the works of perfect Christian virtue spring from love and have no other objective than to arrive at love. (CCC, 25, citing CR, Preface 10)

Quite clearly, then, the *Catechism of the Catholic Church* does not present itself as a new *malleus haereticorum* or as the last word that silences all debate. By its own admission, it is a work in progress, "assembly required." The catechism is thus subject to the same mandate of inculturation that Vatican II imposed on the liturgy itself:

> Even in the liturgy the church does not wish to impose a rigid uniformity in matters which do not involve the faith or the good of the whole community. Rather does it respect and foster the qualities and talents of the various races and nations. Anything in these people's way of life which is not indissolubly bound up with superstition and error it studies with sympathy and, if possible, preserves intact. (SC, 37)

Recognizing Priorities

The new catechism rightly recognizes that "the paschal feasts [are] the origin and center of the Christian liturgy" (CCC, 2042)—even if it buries this crucial insight in small print, in a section dealing with the "precepts of the church" (CCC 2041–43). This is, perhaps, one of several missed opportunities in the catechism as presently structured. For if indeed "the paschal feasts are the origin and center of the Christian liturgy," then one might logically have expected part two of the catechism, "The Celebration of the Christian Mystery," to begin with an evocative mystagogical catechesis based on the rites of the Paschal Triduum, which culminates in the celebration of the sacraments of initiation during the Easter Vigil. This was, in fact, the approach followed in a 1988 document from the Congregation for Divine Worship entitled "Preparing and Celebrating the Paschal Feasts," which begins by noting that:

> [t]he Second Vatican Council repeatedly called attention to Christ's paschal mystery and pointed out that it is the fount from which all sacraments and sacramentals draw their power.
>
> Just as the week has its beginning and climax in the celebration of Sunday, which always has a paschal character, so the summit of the whole liturgical year is in the sacred Easter triduum of the passion and resurrection of the Lord, which is prepared for by the period of Lent and prolonged for fifty days. (#1–2)

Instead of following the lead of this 1988 document—which comments on the actual rites as celebrated by the assembly—the drafters of the catechism chose to define liturgy and explain its significance by means of a "trinitarian model" that resembles the approach of older scholastic manuals of theology. (The title of part two, section 1, chapter 1, article 1 is "The Liturgy—Work of the Holy Trinity.") The impression is given that *doxology* (the rites, words, and symbols of worship) is somehow derived from *doctrine,* rather than the reverse. This impression is reinforced by the fact that the catechism (which deliberately follows the format established by *Catechismus romanus*) places its material on the liturgy *second,* after its exposition of the creed. Thus, although the baptismal (and hence, the *liturgical*) origins of the creed are noted (CCC, 13–14), *the rites themselves* are given rather short shrift. (See CCC, 1234–45.) Important rituals attached to the catechumenate in the RCIA—the presentation of the creed, for instance—are neglected. The document's preoccupation seems to be what is minimally required for validity rather than what is required for a full, conscious, effective celebration by the participating assembly. (See CCC, 1239, and SC, 14, 41, 50; see also the 1967 document *Musicam sacram,* 15: "The faithful fulfill their liturgical role by making that full, conscious and active participation which is demanded by the nature of the liturgy itself and which is, by reason of baptism, the right and duty of the Christian people.")

In adapting the catechism to the conditions of American Catholics (recall the mandate contained in article 24), bishops and other teachers might do well to use the Easter mysteries and their actual liturgical celebration as the *starting point* for catechesis not only about baptism and confirmation but about eucharist as well. For when it comes to the Christian sacraments, the priority is Pascha, not propositions.

Preoccupations

Throughout part two, the catechism seems preoccupied by a need to clarify and explain the *doctrinal* content of the sacraments rather than unfold their rich (and richly ambiguous) ritual, symbolic and mystagogical significance as celebrations of God's people. Although liturgical texts are sometimes quoted, most of the citations in part two (beyond those drawn from scripture) are derived from patristic and theological sources or from magisterial documents. One might have expected more attention to the ritual gestures and prayers that Christians actually use in "celebrating the Mystery." One might have hoped, too, for more attention to the valuable pastoral notes that accompany the revised rites. Recall, for instance, the remarkably balanced theology of human illness and suffering that accompanies the revised rites for anointing the sick. Sickness, the introduction notes, while it is closely related to the human condition, *cannot be considered a punishment which we suffer for our personal sins (Pastoral Care of the Sick,* 2). In this way, the introduction corrects the ancient (and mistaken) linkage between sickness and sin that often results in blaming the victim. Yet this important corrective is passed over in the CCC's discussion of this sacrament. (See CCC 1499–532.) Indeed, the catechism seems to reassert—*against* the contents of the revised rite—the old view that illness is somehow a consequence of sin and evil. (See CCC, 1502.)

The Experience of Believers

Finally, there is the issue of mystagogical catechesis, which, as the catechism rightly notes, is derived from believers' actual experience of liturgical celebration (CCC, 1075). Like the liturgy itself, mystagogy requires cultural adaptation:

> Such catechesis is to be presented *by local and regional catechisms*. This Catechism, which aims to serve the whole Church in all the diversity of her rites and cultures, will present [only] what is fundamental and common to the whole Church in the liturgy as mystery and as celebration. (CCC, 1075; emphasis added)

Here again, the authors of the new catechism seem eager to acknowledge that it is only a beginning, a sketch, an outline to be enlivened and enriched by the cultural diversity that characterizes the people of God. The more daunting tasks of liturgical catechesis and mystagogy are left to "local and regional" efforts. This is an important point, because it means that *pastoral praxis* is *"theologia prima"* (rather than the reverse). It unambiguously asserts that doxology shapes doctrine. It means that *the actual liturgical experience of believers* reveals the basic theological significance of worship and sacrament. It also implies, therefore, that in a decisive sense, the "liturgical portions" of the new catechism have yet to be written.

Eucharistic Theology

A New Approach: Eucharist Is, above All, a Liturgy

In the *New York Times* essay discussed in chapter one, Peter Steinfels comments that "many [American] bishops . . . hope that confusion or ignorance about Catholic beliefs will be countered by the new catechism" (Steinfels 1994, 12[A]). Putting an end to ignorance and ambiguity—especially about the eucharist—was certainly an aim of the Counter Reformation's *Catechismus romanus.* It thus devoted the bulk of its treatise on the eucharist (part two, chapter 4) to detailed doctrinal defenses of correct "matter" and "form" (#12–26) in the sacrament; of the real presence (#27–36); of transubstantiation (#37–46); of the effects and kinds of communion (#47–55); of the dispositions required in the communicant (#56–58); of the obligation to communicate (#59–66); and of the Mass as a sacrifice (#69–80). Only at the end of the chapter—in one brief paragraph—is there any discussion of the eucharist as a *liturgical action* (#81).

But the new *Catechism of the Catholic Church* approaches the eucharist from an entirely different angle. While clearly reaffirming real presence and transubstantiation (#1374–76), it is not as obsessed with these issues as its sixteenth-century predecessor was. Moreover, it contextualizes the discussion of eucharist in ways that distinguish it sharply from the *Catechismus romanus.* First, the catechism places its "treatise on sacraments" *within* the larger section on "The [Liturgical] Celebration of the Christian Mystery" (CCC, part two). Its first question is thus not "What is a sacrament?" (CR, part two, chapter 1, 2) but "Why the liturgy?" (CCC, 1066–68). Secondly, the discussion of eucharist is placed *within* the chapter "The Sacraments of Christian Initiation." The eucharist is thus understood first and foremost as the consummating act of Christian initiation, the climax of the mysteries celebrated at the Easter Vigil. (See CCC, 1212, 1322.) Thirdly, the catechism places its material on sacrifice, presence and sacramental change (#1356–81) *after* its exposition of the eucharist as the action of a liturgical assembly (#1345–55). Hence the eucharist is analyzed first—and properly—as liturgy (#1066, 1068), as icon of the paschal mystery (#1067), as definitive enactment of the economy of salvation (#1333–40), and not as an isolated "object" or "product."

Some Tensions between the Catechism of the Catholic Church and the Reformed Rites

The eucharistic theology offered in the *Catechism of the Catholic Church* is not, therefore, a mere rehash of material from the Tridentine *Catechismus romanus.* On the contrary, the impact of post-conciliar praxis and thought is abundantly evident. (See, for example, CCC, 1345–55, 1368.) Still, there are some places where it is difficult to reconcile the catechism with the church's official liturgical documents. Perhaps the most glaring example involves the bread and cup of the communion rite. Insisting that the faithful should receive communion each time they participate in Mass, the catechism (#1388) repeats *Sacrosanctum concilium*'s dictum that "the more perfect form of participation" (reception of "the Lord's Body from the same sacrifice") is "warmly recommended" (SC, 55). In fact, however, both the 1967 instruction *Eucharisticum mysterium* (EM) and the 1975 edition of the *General Instruction of the Roman Missal* (GIRM) make this point far more strongly than the catechism does:

> In order that the communion may stand out more clearly even through signs as a participation in the sacrifice actually being celebrated, steps should be taken that enable the faithful to receive hosts consecrated at that Mass. (EM, 31)

> It is most desirable that the faithful receive the Lord's body from hosts consecrated at the same Mass. (GIRM, 56h)

These texts insist that the people should communicate from bread consecrated during the eucharist in which they are participating is more than a "warm recommendation" or a casual option that can be dismissed in favor of communion from the reserved sacrament, for what is at stake is nothing less than *the integrity of sacramental signs* (as both EM and GIRM rightly emphasize). Similarly, the catechism (#1390) fudges on the question of communion from the cup. It omits important principles and reverses the order found in the *General Instruction,* which reads:

> Holy communion has a more complete form as a sign when it is received under both kinds. For in this manner of reception a fuller light shines on the sign of the eucharistic banquet. Moreover there is a clearer expression of that will by which the new and everlasting covenant is ratified in the blood of the Lord and of the relationship of the eucharistic banquet to the eschatological banquet in the Father's kingdom. (#240)

[P]astors should instruct the people that according to Catholic faith Christ, whole and entire, as well as the true sacrament are received even under one kind only. (#241)

Note that the *General Instruction* does reaffirm the theory of "concomitance," which states that the whole Christ is present under either species, but only *after* it has affirmed that receiving the cup (1) makes the sacramental sign *more complete*; (2) clarifies the *meaning* of the "eucharistic banquet"; (3) embodies more clearly what *Christ's will* was in establishing the new covenant; (4) shows *how* that covenant was ratified in blood; and (5) demonstrates that the eucharistic meal is a *foretaste* of that feast which awaits us in the kingdom of God.

These are not negligible points. They go to the very heart of the eucharistic celebration as both sacrament and sacrifice. Yet the catechism (#1390) sidesteps the vital (and papally approved!) theology of the *General Instruction* by putting the principle of concomitance in *first* place. Only then does it (rather lamely and reluctantly) admit that the sign of communion is "more complete" when both species are received. Gone is the instruction's emphasis on the theological/ritual connection between eucharistic cup and Jesus' covenant-sealing blood. Gone is the eschatological link between the cup of eucharistic communion and the arrival of God's reign. (See Mark 14:25, Matthew 26:29 and Luke 22:18.) Gone is the potent symbolic relationship between the eucharistic cup and the "cup" of the passion that Jesus embraced freely and fully as God's will.

The catechism's theology of eucharistic communion thus represents a radical impoverishment when compared to the rich collection of insights found in conciliar and post-conciliar sources. If the bishops were hoping that the new catechism would clear up the confusion about the relation between eucharistic doctrine and praxis, they were probably mistaken. By failing to follow the principles carefully enunciated in the approved liturgical books, the catechism actually muddies the waters.

But such lapses are rather rare in the catechism. Its eucharistic theology not only affirms the thought of Vatican II, it expands that thought in some very helpful new directions. Here, attention may be drawn to some of them.

Eucharist and the Poor

The catechism (#1397) offers a bold, succinct summary of the relationship between eucharist and commitment to the poor. This relationship is not a matter of mere homiletic hyperbole, for the catechism declares that truth of receiving Christ's body and blood depends upon recognizing Christ "in the poorest." "You dishonor this table," wrote John Chrysostom, "when you do not judge worthy of sharing your food someone judged worthy to take part in this meal" (Homily on 1 Corinthians 27:4, cited in CCC, 1397). Those marginalized by social and economic injustice not only have a claim on God's mercy but an equally potent claim on the eucharistic community's attention.

Monika Hellwig cogently summarizes the reason for this connection between eucharist and the poor in the second (revised and expanded) edition of her book *The Eucharist and the Hunger of the World:*

> The [eucharist] . . . is in the first place the celebration of the hospitality of God shared by guests who commit themselves to become fellow hosts with God. It is the celebration of the divine hospitality as offered in the human presence of Jesus as word, wisdom and outreach of God. It subsumes in itself the grateful acknowledgment of God's hospitality in creation, but also the recall and renewal of God's liberating intervention on behalf of the *habiru* (Hebrews), the enslaved and deprived who had been kept from peoplehood, freedom and human dignity, and were therefore redemptively called anew to be the People of God, a witness and blessing to all peoples of the earth. (Hellwig 1992, 18)

It is important to point out here that the catechism's welcome affirmation of the indissoluble bond between eucharist and the "preferential option for the poor" represents a significant evolution in the church's theology. If Vatican II marked the return of ecclesiology to eucharistic thought ("the church makes eucharist, and eucharist makes the church"; see SC, 10), the catechism goes a step further by insisting that at Mass we not only "commune with Jesus but with his Kingdom project"; we not only create *church*, we begin to build a new human society (Codina 1993, 671). In other words, the gift of the Risen One

> must become the seed for a new earth and a new heaven, not
> only liturgically but historically (*Gaudium et spes*, 38–39). The
> eucharist is not simply a celebration of small historical victories,
> but a [pledge, a down payment] of the full and final realization
> of the Kingdom of God. Thus [the eucharist] is not only a sub-
> versive memorial (J. B. Metz)—[because it boldly proclaims that
> the present socio-economic order is coming to an end]—but a
> source of hope and the beginning of transfiguration. The bread
> and wine are transformed into bread and wine of the Kingdom,
> the beginning of the final utopia. And Jesus, eschatological medi-
> ator of the Kingdom, is made present with his transforming
> power. The epiclesis is not limited to the transformation of the
> gifts or of the community, but of all history into the body of the
> Lord. (Codina 1993, 672)

So every time Christians gather at the Lord's table, they acknowledge their solidarity with the world's poor, with all the out-cast and marginalized—the unlovely, unloved, unwashed and unwanted of our species—and they also make the radical political statement that the world's present socioeconomic order is doomed. It will, Christians believe, be replaced by God's reign, where all have equal access to the feast, where the only power is power exercised on behalf of the poor and needy, where God's agenda is the human agenda, where God has chosen relatedness to people as the only defi-nition of the divine.

By insisting that the truth of eucharistic participation *depends upon* commitment to the poor (by insisting, in other words, that without *real* sharing there is no Lord's Supper; see 1 Corinthians 11:20–21), the catechism has advanced sacramental theology in at least three basic ways.

First, it has helped us see that the experience of victims, of the marginalized, is not simply a "regrettable social tragedy" but a *locus theologicus,* a source for theology. As Elisabeth Schüssler-Fiorenza has noted, "To truly understand the Bible is to read it through the eyes of the oppressed, since the God who speaks in the Bible is the God of the oppressed" (Schüssler-Fiorenza 1981, 100). A "preferential option for the poor" means giving votes and voices to the *sufferers* of history, to the "losers," to the victims of unjust political and economic systems, to the oppressed, to the "disappeared." It means that theology can no longer be written simply by the "haves"; it must also embrace the experience of the have-nots. For to claim (as CCC, 1397, does) that the sacramental integrity of eucharist depends on recognition of the poor is to say that the oppressed may no longer by treated simply as "objects of social and ecclesial aid" (*power* giving to *need*) but must themselves become "the *active subjects* of their own religious and political history" (Tamayo 1993, 47, emphasis added). In a word, theology can no longer by done with its back turned "to the sufferings of the poor and oppressed of the world" (47).

Second, the bond between eucharist and the poor is rooted in Jesus' vision that voluntary solidarity with the poor and outcast is precisely the *means* and the *manner* in which the reign of God is actualized, made present, in human history. As Jon Sobrino has written:

> Jesus, in the specific historical reality of his life, conceived his mission in such a way that it had to follow a historical course leading inevitably to his being deprived of security, dignity, and life itself—the historical course of voluntary impoverishment. [The gospel shows us a Jesus who is gradually stripped of security, stripped of dignity, stripped of his own life], the true and final impoverishment.
>
> What needs to be stressed in this objective process of impoverishment is that Jesus undertook it out of solidarity with the poor. . . . The five controversies in Mark 2:1—3:5 are based on a *defense* of the sick, sinners, and the hungry. . . . [Jesus'] impoverishment stems from something much deeper than asceticism. It stems from a voluntary solidarity with the poor and outcast.
>
> The requirements Jesus laid on others show that same movement in the direction of basic impoverishment: the call to follow him in order to carry out a mission in poverty, to leave home and family, to take up the cross. . . .
>
> This active process of impoverishment that Jesus practiced in his life is simply the historical version of what was later theologized as his transcendent impoverishment: the incarnation

and *kenosis* (celebrated in the famous hymn in Philippians 2: 6–11). Note that this transcendent impoverishment took historical form *not only* through the assumption of human flesh, but also through the assumption of solidarity with the poor and outcast. (Sobrino 1987, 145–46, emphasis added)

If the eucharist were only a *signum commemorativum,* a remembrance of Jesus' words and deeds, it might be sufficient for the Christian community simply to recall that Jesus voluntarily renounced those patterns of having, holding and hoarding that create inequality, injustice and violence among human beings. But, as Thomas Aquinas understood, the eucharist is also *signum praefigurativum,* an eschatological sign that embodies and effects the life of definitive communion with God *"in patria" (Summa Theologiae,* IIIa.73.4, *corpus).* The eucharist points not merely to past (Jesus' passion) and present (the church's unity) but to the future (God's reign) as well. That future begins arriving—is embodied and enacted—whenever believers voluntarily embrace impoverishment as Jesus did.

Third, this leads to an important point concerning what the new catechism has to say concerning the relation between eucharist and the poor. The challenge, as American Protestant theologian Robert McAfee Brown has noted, is not simply to be "a church of the poor" (Brown, 1979, 342). After all, the church has *always* been that. The vast majority of its members throughout history have *always* been—and still are—plagued by poverty, wretchedness, insecurity, landlessness and injustice. Feeling guilt and sorrow about this situation is not sufficient. Charity is not enough—especially if almsgiving means power giving to need. The challenge, according to Brown, is not to be "a church of the poor" but a "church that is poor," a "poor church." Commenting on the 1979 Puebla document of the Third General Conference of the Latin American Episcopate, "Evangelization in Latin America's Present and Future," Brown writes:

North American Churches, by and large, are the Churches not of the poor but of the middle and upper classes. It is Pentecostals, most black Churches, and some small sect groups who minister to the poor. Mainline Churches do not. . . . Nevertheless, the clear "preferential option" in the Gospel for the poor, to which

Puebla calls attention, is a reality that we North Americans cannot be allowed to ignore. . . . This is not to say that God does not love anybody but the poor . . . even Puebla says that the preferential option is not "exclusive." But if, indeed, God loves the poor first (as Pope John Paul II said in his address to the Barrio of Santa Cecilia 30 January 1979), and sees the poor as the way through whom the Good News can finally be heard by the rich as well, then some reordering and new priorities are mandatory for North American Churches.

This will not be easy. It will mean confronting whether or not we even have the capacity to embrace the notion, let alone act on it. It will mean challenging the economic system by which the Church gains its financial support and which provides the means of livelihood for most of its members, including its pastors. It will mean a radical solidarity with segments of the society that have seldom if ever been within the walls of the Church. . . .

At a post-Puebla conference . . . in Matanzas, Cuba, it was stated that evangelization in our day will go "from the periphery to the center," originating with the *marginalized* in society and going from them toward those with the power. A century ago it was the other way around. The nineteenth century was the "great advance" of missions from the center to the periphery. Perhaps Puebla can be one of the first visible signs of the need to reverse the momentum, signaling that *those in North America who are the non-poor will have to confront what it means to be non-poor in the light of the hard and uncompromising nature of the Gospel.* (342–43, emphasis added)

In sum, in its short paragraph on eucharist and the poor, the catechism suggests a theology of the table that is quite radical and potentially subversive.

Eucharist and Creation

The catechism acknowledges that the eucharist redefines the Christian's relation to the material world. "The whole of creation" is presented to God in the eucharistic sacrifice of praise (CCC, 1359) because it is profoundly implicated in the paschal mystery and shares the resurrection destiny of Christ and the Christian. David Power has emphasized this point beautifully:

The eucharist confirms the doctrine of the one God, creating and redeeming the world through the one Word. It confirms the incarnation, for how could it be offered if the Word had not truly taken on flesh? It confirms the goodness of creation, for how else could God be offered the material things of this earth if they were not God's own? It confirms the resurrection of the flesh, since in it our very bodies are nourished with the flesh and blood of Christ. (Power 1992, 110)

In a profound sense, the eucharist affirms that the world itself is destined to become the very body of God. (See Rahner 1976, 172.)

Eucharist and Spirit

One of the most welcome features of the catechism's eucharistic theology is its recognition of the role of the Spirit:

Christian liturgy not only recalls the events that saved us but actualizes them, makes them present. The Paschal mystery of Christ is celebrated, not repeated. It is the celebrations that are repeated, and in each celebration there is an outpouring of the Holy Spirit that makes the unique mystery present. . . .

[Moreover], in every liturgical action the Holy Spirit is sent in order to bring us into communion with Christ and so to form his Body. . . . The Spirit, who is the Spirit of communion, abides indefectibly in the Church. For this reason the Church is the great sacrament of divine communion which gathers God's scattered children together." (CCC, 1104, 1108)

The catechism also notes that the Spirit's "transforming power" links the assembly's present action with the eschatological "consummation of the mystery of salvation" (CCC, 1107). This is so because "the epiclesis of each sacrament" signifies the Spirit's action "transforming into itself everything it touches" (CCC, 1127, emphasis added).

The "Moment" of Consecration

This renewed attention to pneumatology is also evident in the catechism's more comprehensive theology of eucharistic consecration. For obvious historical reasons, the *Catechismus romanus* was obsessed with the consecratory power of the *verba Domini* to such a degree that the Spirit's role in the consecratory action is utterly ignored. Indeed, its treatise on the eucharist contains not one single reference to the Spirit. (See part two, chapter 4, 1–81.) Such an omission constitutes a serious theological flaw, one the *Catechism of the Catholic Church* is at pains to correct. Thus, the new catechism contains repeated affirmations that the eucharist is consecrated "by the words of Christ *and the invocation of the Holy Spirit*" or "*by the power of the Holy Spirit and* by the words of Christ" (#1333, 1357; see also 1105–6, 1375, 1412). This correction is important because it appreciably broadens our understanding of eucharistic consecration. Although the catechism still uses chronological language to describe this consecration (#1377), it understands that in order to grasp the true significance of liturgical acts, a *non-chronological* view of time is required. The history of salvation—embodied in ritual acts—is *celebration,* not chronology, *meaning,* not mimesis: "The paschal mystery is celebrated, not repeated" (CCC, 1104). God acts *within* time and history but is bound by neither. Mystery cannot be reduced to history. So, too, eucharistic consecration cannot be chronologically compacted into a single "instant." David Power's commentary on the structure of the eucharistic prayer sums it up admirably:

> [T]he supper narrative, the anamnesis, and the epiclesis are in the nature of theological amplifications. They are insertions that give a kind of primary theological explanation of what is being done when Christian people offer praise and thanksgiving over bread and wine in remembrance of Jesus Christ. This affects the disputes about the relative consecratory power of the words of Christ and of the invocation of the Spirit. Neither of these in fact has any significance except in the context of the great prayer and in relation to the act of communion in which the prayer reaches its ritual climax. An analysis of the words of the supper narrative, the anamnesis, and the epiclesis is always helpful to an understanding of the eucharistic action, but the power of the action is not to be identified with any one of them, for they but spell out the meaning of the prayer and action as a whole. (Power 1992, 136)

References to Works Cited in the Text

Brown, Robert McAfee. 1979. "The Significance of Puebla for the Protestant Churches in North America." In *Puebla and Beyond,* edited by John Eagleson and Philip Scharper. Maryknoll, New York: Orbis Books.

Codina, Victor. 1993. "Sacraments." In *Mysterium Liberationis: Fundamental Concepts of Liberation Theology,* edited by I. Ellacuria and J. Sobrino. Maryknoll, New York: Orbis Books.

Hellwig, Monika. 1992. *The Eucharist and the Hunger of the World.* Kansas City: Sheed and Ward.

Power, David. 1992. *The Eucharistic Mystery.* New York: Crossroad.

Rahner, Karl. 1976. "Considerations on the Active Role of the Person in the Sacramental Event." In *Theological Investigations,* vol. 14, translated by Cornelius Ernst. New York: Seabury.

Rodríguez, Pedro, ed. 1989. *Catechismus romanus.* Città del Vaticano: Libreria Editrice Vaticana.

Schüssler-Fiorenza, Elisabeth. 1981. "Toward a Feminist Biblical Hermeneutics: Biblical Interpretation and Liberation Theology." In *The Challenge of Liberation Theology: A First World Response,* edited by B. Mahan and L. D. Richesin. Maryknoll, New York: Orbis.

Sobrino, Jon. 1987. *Jesus in Latin America.* Maryknoll, New York: Orbis Books.

Steinfels, Peter. 1994. "Future of Faith Worries Catholic Leaders." *New York Times,* 1 June 1994.

Tamayo, Juan Jose. 1993. "Reception of the Theology of Liberation." In *Mysterium Liberationis: Fundamental Concepts of Liberation Theology,* edited by I. Ellacuria and J. Sobrino. Maryknoll, New York: Orbis Books.

The Impact of Twentieth-Century Approaches to Scripture for Understanding the Connections between Jesus and Eucharist

Until perhaps the middle of this century, Roman Catholics were often taught that Jesus "instituted" the seven sacraments during his earthly life and ministry, for example, "ordaining" the apostles at the Last Supper while celebrating the "first eucharist" with them. For a variety of reasons, such an image is no longer plausible. Among other things, it ignores the fact that the list of seven sacraments is not scriptural but is rather a product of early medieval theology. This chapter, dealing with the relationship between Jesus and eucharist, will begin by focusing on efforts made by scholars in the last hundred years to clarify the connections between Jesus, the movement that arose in response to his message, and that movement's liturgical life.

Searching for the Historical Jesus

Background

For most of the last century scholars labored to uncover the links between the historical person and work of Jesus (person), Christianity as a religious movement distinct and independent from Judaism (community), and the gospels as biography, hagiography and hermeneutic (text). Scholars have asked: "What are the connections between person, community and text—between the *historical person* of Jesus, the *faith communities* that grew up in response to his ministry, and the *sacred texts* produced by those communities?" To put it another way, research in our century has been preoccupied with the question "Where did christology come from?" Did it begin with Jesus, with claims he himself made about his personal identity, his mission and his relationship with God? Or did it emerge only after Easter, with the New Testament communities and their struggle to make sense of Jesus' execution and subsequent vindication by God in the resurrection? When, how and under what circumstances did christology originate? And does it make any difference to an interpretation of Christian liturgical practices?

For Roman Catholics, this debate began as early as 1902, when Alfred Loisy (a priest and professor at Paris' École Pratique) published a little book entitled *L'Évangile et L'Église*. Loisy's book was a sensationally novel defense of Catholicism written in response to the Protestant exegete and historian Adolf von Harnack, whose 1902 book *Das Wesen des Christentums* attempted to free the "essential and authentic teaching of Jesus" from later dogmatic accretions. Against Harnack, Loisy argued that, in fact, the "essence" of Christianity can be recovered *only from within the developing faith of the church as it unfolds under the guidance of the Spirit*. Loisy freely admitted that while Jesus proclaimed the coming kingdom, what appeared was the church. But the fact that Jesus did not directly "found" a church or "institute" sacraments does not (so Loisy argued) diminish their central role in Christian life.

L'Évangile et l'Église aroused violent responses both for and against it. The archbishop of Paris condemned it, but Rome declined to intervene until after the election of Pius X, who placed the book on the index of forbidden books in 1904. Eventually, Loisy himself resigned his priestly functions and was excommunicated.

In another age, both the book and its author might have remained historical footnotes. But their appearance at the beginning of this century was momentous. Catholicism was ripe for a revolution in biblical, theological and liturgical matters. So in effect, Loisy's book was one of the first shots fired in a long (and often bitter) struggle for theological and pastoral renewal that culminated in the Second Vatican Council.

Postconciliar Theology

After Vatican II, the debates about Christian origins (or more precisely, the origins of christology) intensified. A new stage in the struggle was reached in the late 1970s with the publication of Edward Schillebeeckx's monumental volumes *Jesus* (published in English in 1979) and *Christ* (1980). In many respects Schillebeeckx's work represented the first thorough attempt by a systematic theologian of the Roman Catholic tradition to incorporate the results of serious modern scriptural exegesis into the framework of dogmatic christology. Among many other things, Schillebeeckx reminded readers that the New Testament is not primarily a library of biographies about Jesus, but rather, a collection of literature about the Christian community itself: its origins and mission; its concerns for preaching, catechesis and instruction; its quarrels (internal and external); and its widely varying theological interpretations of Jesus' message, ministry, death and rising (Schillebeeckx 1979, 22). In other words, the *Christian movement itself* is the starting point for reflection about the historical Jesus. We can access the Jesus of history only by pulling together two distinct sets of experiences: what Schillebeeckx calls *pneuma* and *anamnesis,* "spirit" and "memory." *Spirit* refers to the here-and-now experience of Jesus in the faith, daily life, prayer and worship of believers. *Memory* selects and embodies recollections about the "Jesus of the past" that are recorded in the New Testament as stories, sayings, anecdotes, parables, and so on.

Our contact with the historical Jesus is thus always mediated by the belief and practice of a faith-filled community. (Note here the influence of Alfred Loisy's position.) There is no historical magic bullet that can give direct and immediate access to Jesus apart from the community. There is no "Harnackian essence" of Christianity that can be distilled by purely historical means and thus known or affirmed apart from the Spirit-filled lives of believers.

In short, for Schillebeeckx (and, indeed, for the majority of Catholic theologians) *the believing church* is the enveloping "hermeneutic" (the essential interpretive tool) within which christology happens. Even if one claims that christology actually begins with claims Jesus made about himself (the traditional Catholic view), we can know this only within an ecclesiological context. That context is literary and liturgical. In other words, the relation between person, community and text is *anchored* in the authoritative biblical witness— and yet is constantly *renegotiated* in the repeated ritual actions of the assembly. For Catholics, Bible and liturgy are not static, compartmentalized entities but lively, interactive sources of faith that continue throughout history to define one another, comment upon one another and (sometimes) conflict with one another.

To sum it up, for Catholics the sources of christology are multiple. They include Bible, church and worship as these three constantly evoke and challenge one another through those living processes we call "conversion," "faith," the "development of doctrine" and "spiritual growth." The great merit of Schillebeeckx's work is thus to show that christology cannot be held hostage to any single source (as fundamentalists of various types are inclined to do). Our images of Jesus—in the New Testament, in the liturgy, in the church's historical tradition—are richly diverse. No single image or interpretation can account completely for who Jesus is. Still, the gospels remain "privileged sources" and can be said to present a "reflex" of the earthly Jesus within the faith-prompted response of Christians. (See Schillebeeckx 1979, 90.) It is thus possible to use historical-critical methods in order to recover a reasonably accurate picture of who the Jesus of history was and what he taught.

The following points outline some of the prominent features that emerge in Schillebeeckx's portrait of Jesus.

1.   The center of Jesus' preaching is the reign or kingdom of God— defined not as an object, place or program but as the unfolding historical actions, events and processes through which God's being is grasped in and for a world of human persons (rather than as an abstract metaphysical principle). The reign of God for Jesus means that God has chosen "relatedness to persons" as the only definition

of the divine. All other attempts to define God are idle and speculative. God has become Emmanuel: God's being is a being-with-us, a being-for-us. In short, God is that unique "Person" in the universe who "makes a difference to all things, and to whom all things make a difference."

2.   Thus the very nature of God for Jesus is unconditional compassion towards the human world, unimpeachable love for creatures and creation. God is that One who cherishes people and makes them free. God's will is always and only a willing of good. God's power is always and only a power exercised on behalf of those who need it— the poor, the outcast, the despised, the marginalized, the wretched and lonely, the abandoned. God is neither angry nor vengeful precisely because God has no ego to defend.

3.   Jesus thus sees the future as *potential* rather than catastrophe. Jesus' view of time is basically nonchronological. The past is not what the clock has recorded, but rather

> the *reign* of sin and Satan, the *alienation* of people from God, the *weight* of all that is impenetrable to [God's] gift of self. . . . In its place comes the "future," the presence of [God's own self] among those who are living lives of justice and mercy. . . . The name Jesus used for this passing of the ages was "forgiveness." . . . Forgiveness . . . refers not primarily to sin . . . but to the crossing of the eschatological line. What is "given" in [God's] forgiveness is the eschatological future—that is, God's own self. Thus, forgiveness meant the arrival of God in the present, God's superabundant gift of self to people, God's self-communicating incarnation. (Sheehan 1988, 66)

In short, the future is always breaking into this world as *potential,* as justice, as compassion and mercy, as forgiveness. Forgiveness means "crossing the eschatological line." It means the future has become present as potential. It means God is arriving *in this very moment* of human existence. Forgiveness is precisely the act of liberation that frees someone to become God's child.

4.   Through the kind of preaching summarized in the beatitudes, Jesus proclaims the ultimate power of powerlessness (Schillebeecks 1979, 177). God comes not to those who have the right stuff but to those who bottom out. Laughter—not weeping—is the deepest goal God wills for humans. Hence, God's answer to all forms of evil that lead to human misery and suffering is a radical "No!"

5.   In Jesus, praxis cannot be separated from person. God's "cause" is thus revealed as the *human* cause. To put it another way, Jesus is God's hospitality made flesh in the human world. This is especially evident in meal-sharing, a characteristic feature of Jesus' historical ministry that continued in the church after Easter. At table, Jesus is sometimes guest, sometimes host. With sinners and tax collectors, with pariahs and prostitutes, with friends casual and close, Jesus reclines at table. He thus becomes God's invitation to *all* (especially those officially regarded as outcasts) to feast in the kingdom. For Jesus,

> fellowship at table is itself . . . an offer here and now of eschatological salvation. . . . The instances where Jesus himself acts as host bring home even more forcefully the fact that Jesus himself takes the initiative with this eschatological message, which in the fellowship at table . . . becomes . . . an enacted prophecy. (Schillebeeckx 1979, 218)

6.   Jesus' actions (especially at table, but elsewhere, too) are seen by his contemporaries as "wonders," as wonderful, as miraculous. A miracle in the New Testament sense is not a deed that suspends the laws of nature but an action that causes amazement. In the Christian scriptures, faith is the *sine qua non* condition for perceiving God's miraculous power in the human deeds of Jesus of Nazareth. (Thus the evangelist's comment that Jesus could work few wonders in his hometown because the people's faith was so feeble.) In a word, miracles do not produce faith; rather, faith produces miracles.

7.   Finally, in the New Testament, Jesus tells parables and is himself—or becomes—a parable. Defined as stories that defy religious conventions, overturn tradition and subvert the hearer's expectations,

parables can only be "explained" by other parables. In this sense, the cross is the ultimate parable that interprets all the rest.

A Debate Renewed

Although Schillebeeckx escaped the fate of Alfred Loisy, his portrait of Jesus (and its implications for the development of christology and church) aroused considerable controversy and drew fire from Vatican officials. Admittedly, for many North Americans, this christological debate has often seemed academic and European—hence, remote. But all that began to change during the 1980s and 1990s, particularly with the publication of research done by members of the so-called Jesus Seminar (established in 1985 by Robert Funk, John Dominic Crossan and others) and their opponents (representing a more "mainstream" position and including scholars such as John Meier and Raymond Brown). A new dimension was added to the debate when the Pontifical Biblical Commission (PBC) released its remarkable document entitled "The Interpretation of the Bible in the Church." The commission's document is an extremely lucid and sophisticated review of current biblical research and methodology, and substantially affirms the validity and contributions not only of older techniques (for example, historical method, form criticism, redaction criticism) but also of newer, state-of-the-art tools such as rhetorical analysis, narrative analysis, semiotics, the human sciences (sociology, cultural anthropology, psychoanalytic technique) and even feminist hermeneutics.

Still, the distance that separates mainstream Catholic exegetes (Brown, Meier) from those on the left (Funk, Crossan) is great. Two articles published in 1994 reveal how acrimonious this debate about the historical Jesus has become. The first of these appeared in the *National Catholic Reporter* (NCR) under the banner "Who Does the Jesus Seminar Say That I Am?" (26 August 1994, 6–7). The second, which was written by Gerald O'Collins (a professor at the Gregorianum university in Rome) and appeared in *America* magazine, is entitled "What Are They Saying about Jesus Now?" The NCR report is (characteristically) lighter and more informal, highlighting some of the more obvious differences between scholars like Crossan and Meier. The *America* article pays closer attention to the precisely

christological ramifications of the debates about the historical Jesus—
and rather bitterly denounces the methods and conclusions of the
Jesus Seminar (and specifically those of Crossan). As O'Collins analyzes it, the current debate centers on several critical questions:

1.   What claims (if any) did Jesus make about himself? For instance,
did Jesus put himself on a par with God? (See O'Collins 1994, 11.)

2.   Is the revelation about Jesus' identity and role restricted to his
earthly life (11)?

3.   When and under what conditions did claims of Jesus' divinity
emerge? Within Jesus own career? As early as Paul? O'Collins argues
that our earliest Christian writer, Paul, already applies divine titles to
Jesus. But of course one must note that Paul's views were not necessarily those of a majority of early believers, though they later gained
ground (11–12).

4.   How novel or innovative was the idea of a "preexistent divine
person" in the ancient world (10)? Earlier in this century, scholars
were inclined to say it was a rather common notion; today, this view
has been challenged by scholars like James Dunn in *Christology in
the Making* (Philadelphia: Westminster Press, 1980).

5.   What or how much of Jesus' history can/do we know? (See
O'Collins 1994, 13–14.)

6.   How should the gospels be viewed? As a fertile field for historical investigation (as historical records inviting research)? Or are they
"theological/literary wholes" that invite a primarily "religious
response"(14)?

7.   What are the major sources of the synoptic gospel tradition? A
majority of scholars today would answer Mark and "Q" (from the
German *Quelle*, "source"). This is basically a two-source theory. "Q"
refers to what Matthew and Luke have in common over against
Mark, and is thus assumed to be the first (now lost) attempt to put

into writing the teachings of Jesus. It was a sayings collection, however, rather than a gospel.

8.   Who (or what) is the historical Jesus? Obviously this historical Jesus cannot today be known exactly as he was in the first century; allowance must also be made for the later experience of the risen Jesus dwelling in the church. In short, the precise object of Christian faith is not the Jesus of history as reconstructed by scholars. (See Meier 1994, 4–6.) The historical Jesus is that Jesus who is "recoverable or knowable by the means of modern, historical-critical research." But this "critically researched" Jesus cannot, without qualification, be identified with the Jesus Christians encounter in faith, in the church, in sacramental worship.

9.   What criteria of authenticity are needed in order to determine which words and actions actually represent Jesus' historical life? Basing themselves on earlier work (for example, Norman Perrin's *Rediscovering the Teaching of Jesus*), many scholars follow five fundamental criteria:
    (a)   *Criterion of embarrassment.* The church is unlikely to have fabricated an action or saying of Jesus that they would have found embarrassing or uncomfortable. The baptism of Jesus by John the Baptist is an example.
    (b)   *Criterion of discontinuity or dissimilarity.* A saying or action of Jesus is likely to be authentic if it is dissimilar from the Jewish thought of that period or from views of the early church. Jesus' use of an unusual word to address God, *Abba,* exemplifies this criterion. Not only does Jesus use this word, he appears to teach his disciples to do the same. (See Perrin 1967, 40–41). (The view that suggests that *Abba* means "Daddy" has been largely discredited by scholars today; *Abba* was not simply a word used by a child to address a male parent. Still, its use in the Palestinian Judaism of Jesus' day was quite extraordinary—a clue that the usage is probably unique among Jesus and his disciples.)
    (c)   *Criterion of multiple attestation.* A saying or action of Jesus is multiply attested if we have more than one witness to it (not more than one witness in the three synoptics, which have common

sources, but Mark and Paul, for example, or Mark and Josephus). Multiple attestation can also mean that an idea or theme resurfaces in several different forms. For example, the notion of "God's reign" is found not only in *sayings* of Jesus ("If it is by the finger of God that I cast out demons, then the kingdom of God has come to you," [Luke 11:20, Matthew 12:28]), but also in *parables* ("The kingdom of may be compared to . . . ") and *prayer* (the Lord's Prayer).

(d) *Criterion of coherence or consistency.* The issue here is: Does this saying or action fit the pattern that can be discerned in Jesus' ministry? This is the criterion that scholars often use to determine whether a saying attributed to Jesus in a non-canonical source (for example, the gospel of Thomas) may be regarded as authentic. Verse 82 of the gospel of Thomas says, "He that is near me is near the fire; he that is far from me is far from the Kingdom." This saying is probably authentic because, among other things, it rings true with other words of Jesus (see Mark 9:49 and 12:34: "Everyone will be salted with fire"; "You are not far from the kingdom of God"). (See the discussion in Perrin 1967, 44–45.)

(e) *Criterion of Jesus' rejection and execution.* Scholars like John Meier add another criterion: that of Jesus' rejection and death. Obviously what Jesus said and did profoundly disturbed many. It is hard to believe he was simply an early flower-child who traipsed through sunlit fields talking about lilies and love! Who would seek to arrest and execute such a sap? What Jesus said and did was infinitely more threatening.

The cleansing of the temple is almost certainly an action of the historical Jesus. In effect, this deed symbolically shut down Israel's cultic industry and called into radical question a religious institution that claimed unique power to mediate the relationship between God and humanity. Jesus' action would have thrown the priestly aristocracy of Jerusalem (the Sadducees and their allies) into apoplectic rage.

Points of Disagreement: A Summary

In light of the above, it is possible to sketch some of the major differences between those exegetes who are more traditional in their approach to the evolution of christology and those on the left:

MEIER/BROWN	CROSSAN/JESUS SEMINAR
(a) We can uncover the core, the nucleus of history, that lies behind events and personalities in the New Testament.	(a) Does the New Testament present "history remembered" or "prophecy historicized"?
(b) Jesus is the eschatological prophet who looks for a sudden, final eruption of God's rule into the present world. If Jesus is "de-eschatologized," it is difficult to understand why he wold have posed such a threat to his contemporaries.	(b) Jesus was a non-eschatological sage; he was primarily a wisdom teacher.
(c) Meier might be willing to say that process shapes or helps to shape events but would deny that events are simply created by process.	(c) Crossan and others among this group stress the relationship between process and event. Crossan argues that the process of reflecting on the Hebrew scriptures eventually produced those passages in the New Testament that are portrayed as historical (eyewitness) accounts of certain events, Jesus' birth, for example.

Points of Agreement: A Summary

1.   *Fundamentalism/literalism is untenable.* In its 1994 document entitled "The Interpretation of the Bible in the Church," the Pontifical Biblical Commission states:

> The basic problem with fundamentalist interpretation . . . is that, refusing to take into account the historical character of biblical revelation, it makes itself incapable of accepting the full truth of the incarnation itself. . . . It fails to recognize that the word of

God has been formulated in language and expression conditioned by various periods. . . .

The fundamentalist approach is dangerous, for it is attractive to people who look to the Bible for ready answers to the problems of life. It can deceive these people, offering them interpretations that are pious but illusory, instead of telling them that the Bible does not necessarily contain an immediate answer to each and every problem. Without saying as much in so many words, fundamentalism actually invites people to a kind of intellectual suicide. It injects into life a false certitude, for it unwittingly confuses the divine substance of the biblical message with what are in fact its human limitations. (PBC 1994, 510)

Much of the debate about fundamentalism centers on the significance of the so-called literal sense of biblical texts. Both the Pontifical Biblical Commission and the majority of contemporary Catholics exegetes do not understand the phrase "literal sense" in the fundamentalist manner. Rather, as John Meier observes in the NCR article alluded to above, the literal sense is "the sense intended by the original author." (See also PBC 1994, 512.) In the case of Genesis, for example, the literal sense is not the astrophysics or biochemistry of creation, but the author's poetic, religious message—a message about God's relationship to creation, about the meaning of the sabbath, about the place of humankind in a creation willed by God. In short, the literal sense of Genesis would be something like this: Creation invites us to relationship with God. This is God's plan. Creation itself is a complex reality in which we humans can be free and responsible. God creates by making this world of freedom and responsibility possible for men and women. Fundamentalists actually distort the literal sense of Genesis by insisting that its authors were trying to teach history, science or the "divine chemistry" that led to the beginning of the universe.

The Pontifical Biblical Commission rejects the fundamentalist view quite unambiguously:

The literal sense is not to be confused with the "literalist" sense to which fundamentalists are attached. It is not sufficient to translate a text word for word in order to obtain its literal sense. . . .

When it is a question of a story, the literal sense does not necessarily imply belief that the facts recounted actually took place, for a story need not belong to the genre of history but [may] be instead a work of imaginative fiction. (PBC 1994, 512)

2. *Jesus must be understood as a person of his time and culture.* Full-bodied faith in the incarnation requires that Jesus be seen as not only truly human but also as truly historical—as a real citizen who participated in the life, economy and sociopolitical institutions of the ancient Mediterranean world. That world, we know today, was dominated (as ours is) by specific and identifiable cultural ideologies. That is why the Pontifical Biblical Commission explicitly commends research in the human sciences, especially sociology and cultural anthropology (PBC 1994, 506–7). Such research provides us with a much better understanding of the world in which Jesus lived. Commenting on recent studies of first-century Mediterranean societies (used by Crossan and others), the commission comments:

> Cultural anthropology seeks to define the characteristics of different kinds of human beings in their social context—as, for example, the "Mediterranean person"—with all that this involves by way of studying the rural or urban context and with attention paid to the values recognized by the society in question (honor and dishonor, secrecy, keeping faith, tradition, kinds of education and schooling), to the manner in which social control is exercised, to the ideas which people have of family, house, kin, to the situation of women, to institutionalized dualities (patron-client, owner-tenant, benefactor-beneficiary, free person–slave), taking into account also the prevailing conception of the sacred and the profane, taboos, rites of passage from one state to another, magic, the source of wealth, of power, of information, etc. . . .
>
> This kind of study can be useful for the interpretation of biblical texts. . . . In the texts which report the teaching of Jesus, for example the parables, many details can be explained thanks to this approach. This is also the case with regard to fundamental ideas, such as that of the reign of God or of the way of conceiving time with respect to the history of salvation, as well as the processes by which the first Christians came to gather in communities. (507)

3. *The focus of Jesus' preaching is the kingdom or reign of God.*
Virtually all scholars today, both Catholics and Protestants of the left,
right and center, agree that the reign of God is absolutely central to
Jesus' career as preacher and prophet. Perhaps the classic modern formulation of this point is that of Norman Perrin:

> The central aspect of the teaching of Jesus was that concerning
> the Kingdom of God. Of this there can be no doubt and today
> no scholar does, in fact, doubt it. Jesus appeared as one who
> proclaimed the Kingdom; all else in his message and ministry
> serves a function in relation to that proclamation and derives its
> meaning from it. (Perrin 1967, 54)

This kingdom (or, better, reign) is not a place or a thing but a
deed. It is a verb, not a noun.

> The kingdom of God is the power of God expressed in deeds; it
> is that which God does wherein it becomes evident that [God] is
> king. It is not a place or community ruled by God; it is not even
> the abstract idea of reign or kingship of God. It is quite con-
> cretely the activity of God as king. (Perrin 1967, 55)

As the Catholic exegete Rudolf Schnackenburg expressed it, God's
rule "is characterized not by latent authority but by the exercise of
power, not by an office but a function. It is not a title but a deed"
(Schnackenburg 1963, 13).

There is, however, some debate among scholars today over
whether Jesus' view of God's reign was eschatological. Was Jesus
awaiting a future intervention of God in history? Or was his teaching
centered on the actual arrival of that future *now,* in this present
moment of a person's existence? Scholars like Perrin emphasize the
eschatological character of Jesus' message. Jesus "proclaimed the
eschatological Kingdom of God . . . a future act of God which will be
decisive for the salvation of the people . . . the last and completely
effective act . . . an all-transforming act of God on behalf of people
(Perrin 1967, 56).

This eschatological thrust of Jesus' preaching is also affirmed
by scholars like John Meier. An alternative view, however, is represented by Thomas Sheehan, who suggests that a more accurate way

to portray Jesus' view is to speak of the "future-present." He argues that Jesus' view of time was basically nonchronological. The past and the future are not points on a time line but

> eschatological categories that had to be read in terms of the only thing that mattered to Jesus: the presence of God-with-us. . . .
>
> The "past" was the reign of sin and Satan, the alienation of people from God, the weight of all that was impenetrable to [God's] gift of self. . . . In its place came the "future," the presence of [God's own self] among those who lived lives of justice and mercy. . . . The name Jesus used for this passing of the ages was "forgiveness." . . . Forgiveness . . . referred not primarily to sin . . . , but to the crossing of the eschatological line. What was "given" in [God's] forgiveness was the eschatological future— that is, God's own self. Thus, forgiveness meant the arrival of God in the present, God's superabundant gift of self to people, God's self-communicating incarnation. (Sheehan 1986, 66)

4. *The Jesus of history "is not and cannot be the object of Christian faith"* (Meier 1991, 197). For centuries, Christians believed in Jesus Christ without having much access to historical sources, and certainly without the benefit of modern historical-critical tools— *Formgeschicte, Redaktionsgeschicte,* and so on. Yet we cannot deny their faith was real and deep. Moreover, the historical Jesus is always a reconstruction to some degree. The question becomes, then: Whose reconstruction is to be accepted? Albert Schweitzer's? Rudolf Bultmann's? Günther Bornkamm's?

Obviously, "the proper object of Christian faith is not and cannot be an idea or scholarly reconstruction, however reliable." John Meier makes this point forcefully:

> For the believer, the object of Christian faith is a living person, Jesus Christ, who fully entered into a true human existence on earth in the first century CE, but who now lives, risen and glorified, forever in the Father's presence. Primarily, Christian faith affirms and adheres to this person—indeed, incarnate, crucified, and risen—and only secondarily to ideas and affirmations about him. In the realm of faith and theology, the "real Jesus," the only Jesus existing and living now, is this risen Lord, to whom access is governed only through faith. (198)

5. Still, the Jesus of history remains important for Christian theology. "The historical Jesus, while not the object or essence of *faith*, must be an integral part of modern *theology*" (Meier 1991, 198–99). This is the case for at least four reasons:

(a) Jesus is not—and was not—a mythic symbol or a timeless archetype. "Christian faith is the affirmation of and adherence to a *particular* person who said and did *particular* things in a *particular* time and place in human history" (199, emphasis added). The structure of Christian faith is inescapably historical. It is also incarnational. When it comes to the Jesus of history, Christians believe in the scandal of particularity.

(b) The real humanity of Jesus continues to be an integral part of Christian faith. Orthodox Christians are not Monophysites. They affirm that the risen Jesus is "the same person who lived and died as a Jew in first-century Palestine, a person as truly and fully human— with all the galling limitations that involves—as any other human being" (199).

(c) The quest for the historical Jesus has helped Christians avoid the temptation to domesticate Jesus within a comfortable, respectable, bourgeois Christianity. For this reason the quest for the historical Jesus has often emphasized the "embarrassing, nonconformist aspects of Jesus; for example, his association with the religious and social 'lowlife' of Palestine, his prophetic critique of external religious observances . . . his opposition to certain religious authorities, especially the Jerusalem priesthood" (199).

(d) The historical Jesus cannot be easily co-opted by or for any particular cause or movement.

> Compared with the classical prophets of Israel, the historical Jesus is remarkably silent on many of the burning social and political issues of his day. He can be turned into a this-worldly political revolutionary only by contorted exegesis and special pleading. Like good sociology, the historical Jesus subverts not just some ideologies but all ideologies. (199)

In other words, Jesus refuses to fit any of our constructed categories. Jesus' importance is precisely that he is strange, off-putting, embarrassing and offensive to all parties—both the left and the right.

"The more we appreciate what Jesus meant in his own time and place, the more 'alien' he will seem to us" (200).

6. *The Jesus of faith is the Risen One, but resurrection must not be confused with resuscitation.* As the *Catechism of the Catholic Church* (CCC) remarks:

> Christ's Resurrection was not a return to earthly life, as was the case with the raisings from the dead that he had performed before Easter: Jairus' daughter, the young man of Naim, Lazarus. These actions were miraculous events, but the persons miraculously raised returned by Jesus' power to ordinary earthly life. At some particular moment they would die again. Christ's Resurrection is essentially different. In his risen body he passes from the state of death to another life beyond time and space. At Jesus' Resurrection his body is filled with the power of the Holy Spirit: he shares the divine life in his glorious state, so that St. Paul can say that Christ is "the man of heaven."(CCC, 646; 1 Corinthians 15:35–50)

When speaking about Easter, therefore, several things have to be borne in mind:

(a) No one witnessed Jesus' resurrection. No one saw it happen. It was not perceptible by the senses. No evangelist describes it. No one can say how it happened "physically." (See CCC, 647.)

(b) Although Easter is historical in the sense that its effects can be described (especially its impact on the spice-bearing women—see Mark 16:8—and on the disciples, who had previously fled and abandoned Jesus at his most critical moment), it is not an event that occurs *within* history (in the way, for example, that someone's birthday does). Rather, as the catechism aptly puts it, Easter "remains at the very heart of the mystery of faith as something that transcends and surpasses history" (CCC, 647).

(c) In the New Testament, resurrection is a transformation, not a resuscitation. Such a transformation is not necessarily incompatible with the irreversible process of dissolution that begins immediately after human death (otherwise we would have trouble affirming the resurrection destiny of Christians, which the Apostles' Creed and the Nicene Creed affirm). Among Palestinian Jews of Jesus' time there was a rather widely held conviction that, at the end of time, the dead would rise. But that resurrection was understood in an eschatological rather than a narrowly physical sense. For a Palestinian Jewish believer to say "Jesus has been raised from the dead" was thus not to declare some fact about the biochemical fate of Jesus' body/person but to affirm the conclusion that the new eschatological era has definitively arrived. Believers are thereby challenged to join themselves with their risen Lord to this end time through conversion, faith and baptism.

(d)   Resurrection thus signifies the dawning of a new and definitive age, the arrival of the eschatological era, with its promise of a new relation between God and humanity (one based on the experience of forgiveness).

(e)   The quality of the life of the resurrection is thus utterly different from the life we now live. This is precisely Paul's argument in 1 Corinthians 15:42–43 and 15:52–54.

(f)   While the New Testament assumes there is a continuity between the earthly Jesus and the transformed Risen One, it is also convinced that this continuity cannot instantly be perceived, even by people who knew Jesus well. Thus Jesus is unrecognizable to the disciples on the road to Emmaus (Luke 24:16) or along the seashore (John 20:14; 21:4). He appears "in another form" (Mark 16:12).

(g)   In the New Testament, the most primitive references to Jesus' resurrection (those found in Paul's letters) do not involve an empty tomb. (See 1 Corinthians 15:3–8.) Rather, Paul speaks of Jesus' *appearances* to believers. According to 1 Corinthians 15: 5–11, "[Christ] appeared [first] to Cephas, then to the twelve. Then he appeared to more than five hundred brothers and sisters at one time . . . . Then he appeared to James, then to all the apostles. Last of all . . . he appeared also to me." It should be observed that this list is both interesting and problematic. Was not Cephas one of the Twelve? Why does Paul not say "to Cephas *and the rest of* the Twelve"? Why is James—the esteemed head of the Jerusalem church—so far down on the list? Is this a hint that Paul considers him inferior or second-rate? Note, too, that Paul does not identify "the Twelve" with "the apostles." Note further that Paul is careful to include himself in the appearances list—thereby validating his own claim as apostle and privileged witness to Jesus' resurrection. Note finally that Paul appears to be quoting—and at the same time *glossing*—an already traditional formula. In any case, Paul either did not know the empty tomb tradition or did not think it had to be mentioned in order to affirm Jesus' resurrection.

(h)   These facts about the earliest Easter traditions have led scholars like Edward Schillebeeckx to observe that in the New Testament the most important thing about Easter is not what happened to *Jesus* but what happened to *the disciples*. The Easter stories are, above all, stories of the disciples' conversion, of their experience of forgiveness and vocation, of coming together as church. Conversion is tied to "seeing the Lord," an event that often occurs in the context of ritual meals. So the experience of conversion is usually described as *communal,* as *eucharistic* and as *graced* (the result of a gracious initiative by God). (As many scholars today note, much of the Easter material deals with questions of authority and precedence in the community, as in Paul's careful ranking of those who received appearances from the Risen One above, and with questions of church foundation and liturgy, as in Matthew 28:19, "Go . . . make disciples of all nations, baptizing them . . ."

(i)   The empty tomb stories in the New Testament are never presented as apologetic proofs of the resurrection. The tomb does not explain the resurrection but rather *the resurrection explains the tomb.* Of itself the tomb produces not faith but fear and confusion (see Mark 16:8). The empty tomb is thus never seen in the New Testament as a source of faith. That source lies elsewhere. For believers, Easter faith has its roots not in some historical past but in an eschatological present-future, what Jesus referred to as God's reign, what Mark's gospel links to the parousia, when Jesus' victory will be fully revealed.

In sum, in the New Testament sources the emptiness of the tomb originally has no Easter meaning. Rather, that emptiness was a terrifying source of confusion and silence. Indeed, in the New Testament traditions, an angel (an apocalyptic messenger) is assigned to the tomb precisely in order to explain that Jesus has been raised (and so has "gone away," gone elsewhere). Furthermore, in Mark's gospel, the event that evokes faith is Jesus' death on the cross, not its aftermath the next Sunday morning. Indeed if (as virtually all scholars agree) Mark's gospel originally ended at chapter 16, verse 8, then Mark would seem to negate a visible resurrection altogether, instead rewriting the tradition about it back into his account of the transfiguration at Mark 9:2–8. This is in line with Mark's powerful theology of the cross, and is also in line with his view that Jesus' glory and victory will be manifest only *hereafter,* in the parousia. For Mark, Christians are not an Easter people and alleluia is not their song. Rather, Christians live in a time of absence and deprivation—Jesus is *gone!* They must imitate their Lord by waiting patiently in faith and suffering until God reveals the future glory.

(j) All this shows that twentieth-century preoccupations about Easter are not necessarily those of the gospels. The modern obsession centers on the tomb's contents (or lack thereof). But in the accounts of the synoptic gospels, the more important theme is the *seeking* that prompts the women disciples (and later the men) to come to the tomb in the first place. The word "seek" always appears in the gospel accounts of the empty tomb, and, indeed, it always comes before any mention of the resurrection or the appearances of Jesus. Seeking is thus inseparable from whatever Easter is and means. Indeed, the New Testament suggests that Easter happens only for those who are truly seeking. Thus, Easter is not so much a past historical event as *an ongoing hermeneutical and experiential task.*

To interpret Easter as a seeking is not, of course, to deny that Jesus' resurrection really occurred. After all, no one seeks for something—or someone—who is utterly absent or unknowable. Indeed, seeking implies that what is sought can somehow be known, felt and experienced. As Thomas Sheehan has observed:

> All seeking is initiated and guided by the absent as seekable, something desired but not possessed, something guessed at but not fully known, something partially present in its absence. . . .
>
> Such seeking is not something we occasionally get caught up in; rather it is what makes us human, constitutes us as the futile passion, the unfulfilled and presumably unfulfillable desire that we are. If we were not this endless eros, either we would be God, who [by definition] . . . cannot seek, or we would be animals, those living entities that lack an "ontological imagination"

and therefore never have a desire that exceeds the possibility of being fulfilled.

This fundamental desire, this seeking that constitutes human nature . . . refuses to be quenched. It dwells like a ghost in the rooms of our everyday lives, haunting all our doings with the dream of the impossible. Thus, beyond all our seeking for things that can be found . . . we find ourselves still directed to a "more" that does not exist. We remain, fundamentally, an act of questioning to which there is no answer. We [remain] an endless and unfulfillable seeking. (Sheehan 1988, 168, 172)

Eucharistic and Sacramental Traditions in the New Testament

Introduction

As noted at the beginning of this chapter, it is no longer possible to affirm without qualification that during his historical life Jesus consciously and explicitly instituted sacraments like baptism or eucharist. The New Testament itself does not, for example, possess a single eucharistic tradition. John's gospel doesn't even include a eucharistic institution account but instead replaces it with the act of foot washing. Or take the notion that Jesus commanded Christians to repeat his actions at the "Last Supper." Paul quotes a tradition in which Jesus says, "Do this in remembrance of me," but none of the synoptics except Luke contain a command to repeat Jesus' actions. (See 1 Corinthians 11:23–26; Luke 22:19.) A number of Catholic exegetes today, therefore, argue that the core of Jesus' eucharistic teaching should be sought not in the Last Supper accounts but elsewhere in the New Testament.

An Example: The Meals in Mark's Gospel

An example of this newer approach appears in the extremely interesting doctoral dissertation written in 1988 by Lee Edward Klosinski on *The Meals in Mark*. Several points in Klosinski's analysis merit careful attention.

1. *Context*. Klosinski first notes the importance of context in Mark. Today it is a commonplace among exegetes to note that Mark's gospel is a story of progressive incomprehension on the part of Jesus' disciples, his closest (male) associates. Failure and flight characterize their reactions to Jesus' arrest, trial and passion. Thus, it comes as no surprise that, in Mark, the witnesses at the empty tomb are women. No male disciple is present at all. As a group, the disciples in Mark come off badly. Their faith is weak, their comprehension slight, their courage feeble, and their lack of awareness appalling. They are unable to grasp the central fact about Jesus' identity: that he is God's martyred prophet, that the cross is the pivot of God's plan for the world's salvation. (Note that the person who ultimately does understand Jesus' identity—and confesses it at the foot of the cross—is not a disciple or a devout Jew or a Gentile Christian but a Roman centurion, a pagan, an unbeliever, one of the enemy.)

A related point of context involves Mark's concern for egalitarianism and inclusivity, especially in matters dealing with food and table fellowship. Thus, in Mark 7:18–20 (see also 7:15–16), Jesus argues forcefully that food taboos have no meaning or merit, that one cannot use food to evaluate a person's moral integrity or religious devotion. "Whatever enters a person from outside cannot defile, but the things that come out are what defile." In the ancient Mediterranean world, of course, this would have been an astonishing pronouncement—for in that culture, *what* one eats, *how* one eats and *with whom* one eats are essential clues to social rank, status and power. Every table, every meal, celebrated the virtues of social hierarchy and class distinctions. The table (and the rituals that happened there) had thus become complex metaphors for social control, for gauging social standing, for determining religious allegiance. By declaring all foods clean and by insisting that *everyone* was welcome at *every table,* Jesus taught that the natural bounty of the world (its animals, its vegetable produce, its people) could no longer be used to hold the hungry hostage or to engineer perverse systems of social oppression.

To challenge what was done at table (by arguing, as Jesus does, that one can eat *anything* with *anyone* at *any time*) is thus to subvert the very basis of Mediterranean sociopolitical life. And that, according to Mark, is exactly what Jesus did.

2.   *"Last Supper" or final betrayal?* Thus what is at stake in Jesus' table ministry for Mark is the very nature of our relationships with God, with others and with the world. The focus is not what's on the table but who's at the table. The Last Supper, as Mark tells it, is not a beautiful tale about Jesus offering himself to others as food and drink but a scandalous story of stupidity and cowardice on the part of those who should have known better. The Last Supper in Mark is less an institution than an indictment. It is not so much a sacramental event as a final proof of failure that reaches its climax when one of the disciples' own number is tagged as Jesus' betrayer (Mark 14:17ff).

Note that in Mark Jesus announces his imminent betrayal as soon as the group is assembled, *before* the meal has even begun. Luke redacts the scene considerably, identifying the betrayer only *after* the meal. Moreover, Mark makes it quite clear that *all* Jesus' disciples are implicated in this act of denial and treachery. There are neither innocents nor autocrats at the table in Mark's account: The same food is distributed to all alike, without distinction, and all twelve disciples drink from the same cup. As Klosinski notes, there is bitter irony in this innocent scene of cup-sharing, for it proves that all Jesus' companions are party to his betrayal. All share equal responsibility for failure, and all will share equally in the cross ("cup" is code in Mark for both Jesus' and the community's passion and suffering). For Mark, the scene at the table is truly and totally egalitarian. It signals not only the end of all religious autocracies but also that the life and death of each disciple is inextricably bound to the life and death of all.

Ironically, then, Mark does not identify the (male) disciples as faithful custodians of eucharistic tradition; rather, he sees them as bunglers whose obtuseness and cowardice lead directly to their master's capture by his enemies. It is thus quite possible that Mark's account of the Last Supper was constructed not so much to commemorate eucharistic origins as to condemn the disciples' failure and to criticize those later Christians (that is, Mark's own contemporaries) whose ritual meals fail to reflect Jesus' revolutionary emphasis on egalitarianism and inclusivity.

3.   *The table of God's bounty.* Klosinski thus argues that the heart of Mark's eucharistic doctrine is not found in the Last Supper scene, but in the stories of Jesus' miraculous multiplication of loaves and fishes. Significantly, the only miracle found in all four gospels is one involving food: the story of Jesus' feeding the multitudes (Mark 6:34–44, Matthew 14:13–21, Luke 9:10b–17, John 6:1–15). It is obvious that the evangelists (each in his own distinctive way) saw a link between the miraculous multiplication of loaves and fishes, and the traditions of Christian eucharist (note the "took, blessed, broke, gave" language of the feeding stories). Klosinksi has suggested that "this juxtaposition of miracle and eucharist" is a parabolic maneuver designed to shake hearers/readers into new ways of thinking about both miraculous deeds and eucharistic fellowship (Klosinski 1988, 176).

There are two keys to this parabolic rethinking. The first is the unusual nature of Jesus' deed—multiplying *food*—for although miracle stories were common stock in the ancient world, virtually none of them ever took the miraculous multiplication of food as a theme. The second key is *extravagance*—the huge crowd, the small number of loaves and fishes, yet the resulting satisfaction of the hungry: "[A]ll ate and were filled" (Mark 6:42). This combination of strange theme and extravagant result stretches the boundaries of the real and the possible to the breaking point. Moreover, from the reader's viewpoint, the story's decisive element—just how Jesus accomplished this extraordinary feat—is never described! Readers are required to supply their own conclusions about the manner in which the miracle was accomplished.

Further complicating matters for the reader is the presence of familiar eucharistic language in the story. Jesus "*taking* the five loaves . . . *blessed* and *broke* the loaves and *gave* them . . ." (Mark 6:41). The reader naturally begins wondering what the connections are between this miraculous multiplication of food and the eucharistic meals of the community, which is exactly the point of the story's parabolic strategy. As virtually all scholars agree, one can already discern in the New Testament itself a movement away from concern about community meals to concern with cultic moments and cultic elements (most specifically, with the elements of bread and wine identified with Jesus' body and blood, interpreted in terms of his saving death for all). But by repeating the "taking, blessing, breaking, giving" language in the miraculous feeding stories, the evangelists have redirected attention to the meaning of Jesus' other meals (and not just the Last Supper). Indeed, Mark's redirection of attention to the eucharistic significance of "loaves and fishes" is even more emphatic, since for him the Last Supper is not meant to be a repeated event but rather is, as noted above, the culmination of his theme about the disciples' failure to understand and an interpretation of Jesus' death in light of the martyrological tradition as a saving event. (See Klosinski 1988, 202.)

This bringing together of diverse elements—a bizarre story, an incredibly extravagant deed done within a eucharistic atmosphere—thus creates a parabolic conflict that requires readers to relinquish their exclusive focus on the highly cultic images of the Last Supper and to redirect attention to the memory and meaning of those meals in which Jesus fed the hungry and responded immediately to real human needs through the extravagant gesture of the multiplication of loaves and fishes. In other words, these stories challenge Christians to remember that eucharistic origins lie not in Jesus' *last* meal but in *all* those events wherein Jesus (as guest or host) satisfied hunger, announced the unbridled joy of God's arrival in the present moment (God's reign), and offered healing and hope to the poor and needy.

A similar challenge occurs in stories like that of the Jesus' anointing at Bethany (Mark 14:3–9). In this story, too, readers are confronted by an outrageous and extravagant situation. Jesus is at table in the home of a *leper*, when a *woman* bearing an alabaster jar of expensive perfume comes to him. Taking the jar, she breaks it and pours the perfume on Jesus' head (note the "taking/breaking/giving" language). Note well that Mark's story of the Last Supper contains no command to repeat it, but *this* story, of a *woman's* extravagant gesture of hospitality in the context of a *meal,* is to be repeated "wherever the gospel is proclaimed . . . in remembrance of *her.*" The point is unmistakable. The woman's extravagant deed of service and love is the true meaning of eucharistic dining (as opposed to the greed and narrow-minded bickering of the onlookers in the story). (See Klosinski 1988, 120.)

In Mark's view, "Do this in memory of me" means "Do this in memory of *her*. Make your eucharistic table a place of lavish abundance and extravagant service, where the tired, the poor, the hungry, and all who are driven by despair and need may find real food, real rest, real comfort, real nurture." Indeed, it is the abundant presence of these things that signals the presence of Jesus, of God, as table partner. Perhaps it is time for us to wonder if our essentially *cultic* eucharist has not blinded us to its broader and more basic meaning. As church historian Peter Brown has noted, one of the most far-reaching decisions in religious history was Christianity's choice to abandon a eucharist of abundance in favor of one that stressed symbolic elements. (See citation in Crossan 1991, 366–67.) Christianity chose, in short, a meal that placed interpersonal bonding ahead of access to food and drink. It may thus prove beneficial to take another look at the multiplication of loaves and fishes. In Brown's words:

> A Christian church, patronized largely by the well-fed and increasingly led by austere men . . . whose restricted diet was the result of choice and not of necessity, found itself, in the next centuries, increasingly tempted to treat sexuality (a drive which frequently assumes leisure and regular eating habits), rather than greed and greed's dark shadow in a world of limited resources and famine, as the most abiding and disquieting symptom of the frailty of the human condition. Maybe the time has come to look again at the seemingly absurd dreams of abundance of ancient Mediterranean men, to find, through their concerns, one way, at least, to more humane and more commonsensical objects of anxiety. (Crossan 1991, 367)

As Christian history unfolded, then, attention shifted. Jesus' focus on open companionship at table (a meal practice that emphasized radical egalitarianism, inclusivity and abundance) was replaced by a focus on the presence of Jesus himself. *The bread-breaker became the bread broken.* Concern for cultic moments and cultic elements replaced concern for "feeding the five thousand," for multiplying loaves and fishes on behalf of the hungry. Gradually the community meal itself (as a time of joyful assembly, feasting, care of the needy and instruction) assumed less importance, and a cultic eucharistic meal (with emphasis on the bread and cup as Christ's body and blood) grew ever more significant. (This eucharistic tradition was already familiar to Paul, who links the elements of broken bread and poured-out wine to Jesus' saving death.) Perhaps the challenge today is to do as Mark did: to refocus our understanding of the Last Supper by relocating its eucharistic significance in the meals through which Jesus brought real food to the hungry, real healing to the sick and real rest to the weary.

Interpreting the New Testament Data: Some Points to Bear in Mind

The material just now summarized suggests some rules of thumb that ought to be borne in mind whenever we deal with what the New Testament teaches about eucharist or sacramental realities.

1.   *Sacramental participation.* In the New Testament, the primary sacramental question does not seem to be "How is Jesus present in the species of bread and wine?" but rather "How does a Christian participate in Christ?" This is the question that preoccupied Christianity's earliest sacramental theologian, Paul.

(a)   *Participation through faith.* For Paul, the answer to the second question is simple and basic. The primary mode of participating in Christ is *faith*. And faith is a response to a proclamation, to a spoken word. Hearing is thus the event that awakens faith. And hearing leads to heeding; faith leads to obedience. (See Romans 1:5, "the obedience of faith.") For Paul the gospel is a message that makes a decisive claim on the hearer. It calls for a response that is not only intellectual but moral. (It may be noted here that this notion of faith as the primary mode of participating in Christ continued in the Christian tradition. It shaped Augustine's famous dictum, found in his commentary on John's gospel, *"Crede, et manducasti,"* a formula that the Reformers made much of during the sixteenth century.)

(b)   *Participation in Christ* through baptism and eucharist. Paul believed that Christians also participate in Christ through baptism and eucharist. An earlier generation of scholars felt that Paul's sacramentalism reflected the influence of Hellenistic mystery cults (participation by believers in a dying and rising deity). Today, such influence is largely discounted by exegetes. As Leander Keck has written,

> Participation in Christ was not [for Paul] a "mystical experience" of conscious identification or absorption into Christ. The accent was not on consciousness at all or on "religious experience," but rather on the "objective transference into a domain of power." To be baptized into Christ is to be included in the domain of Christ, his field of force. (Keck 1979, 57–58)

In other words, Paul was perhaps alluding to what later Catholic tradition described as "objective efficacy," which describes an event whose power does not depend on the feelings or personal dispositions of participants. It is important to note, however, that when Paul argued that "all of us who have been baptized into Christ Jesus were baptized into his death" (Romans 6:3) he did not mean that the ritual washing somehow makes the past event of Christ's dying present to the individual. Rather, *it is the other way around.* The individual is made present to—becomes a participant in— Christ's death. (See Keck 1979, 58.) For Paul, it is not a matter of making the Christ-event present to the believer; it is a matter of making the believer present to the Christ-event through grace, faith and the Spirit. It is not a matter of making Jesus' lordship present to the church, but of making the church present to Jesus' lordship.

Similarly, for Paul participation in Christ through the eucharist means recognizing that the Lord's body is not only on the table but at the table. (See 1 Corinthians 11:29.) The meal not only brings believers into the domain of Christ's death; it also implicates them in each other's lives.

2.   *Deutero-Pauline developments.* Paul himself never used the word "mystery" to refer to sacramental rites such as baptism or eucharist. But deutero-Pauline material does move in that direction. Perhaps the most obvious example is the application of sacramental or mystery language to the relationship that exists between Christ and the church, and between husbands and wives in Ephesians 5:32. The Greek text calls this set of parallel relationships *mysterion mega*

(to mysterion touto mega estin), which the Latin Vulgate translated as *sacramentum magnum*.

Another example occurs in the pastoral literature of the New Testament, specifically Titus 3:5, with its reference to the "water of rebirth," a phrase not found in Paul's authentic letters. Paul himself did not say that baptism is a rebirth for Christians; he did not use the "born again" vocabulary of John's Nicodemus story (John 3:1–21). Rather, he argued that baptism makes believers present to—and thus participants in—the death of Christ, and so enables them to "walk in newness of life" (Romans 6:4).

3.   *Pauline sacramentalism.* What we have in Paul's own writings might be called an ecclesiological sacramentalism. Paul did not try to root the community's rituals (baptism, Lord's Supper) in any command of the historical Jesus. Indeed, as many exegetes observe, Paul was almost totally uninterested in the events of Jesus' earthly existence. What interested Paul was *the risen Lord who assembles a church*. Baptism and eucharist were thus seen as *ecclesial* actions that bring the assembly (through faith, grace, and the Spirit) into participation with Christ's death, with the risen life he now lives in God's presence. Even the Lord's Supper, though based on deeds of the historical Jesus (see the tradition Paul cites in 1 Corinthians 11:23–26), derives its meaning from Jesus' *death*—and from the community's recognition that Christ is not only *on* the table but *at* and *around* the table. Hence Paul's favorite image for the assembly was *"soma tou Christou,"* "body of Christ" (1 Corinthians 12:27).

4.   *Johannine sacramentalism.* Unlike Paul, for whom Jesus' earthly career was largely a matter of indifference, John's gospel sought to locate the source of sacraments in the *earthly* life and career of Jesus. It must be remembered that for John, the historical Jesus was none other than the preexistent Logos, the divine person who is always "one with the Father." It should thus be remembered that John's sacramentalism (especially his allusions to eucharist) was designed to highlight the reality of the incarnation. In this evangelist's view, questions about Jesus' true identity were more theologically fundamental than questions about the proper interpretation of baptism or

eucharist, though in practice the two questions are closely related. The crucial point for John was that participation in sacraments is designed to show both the *reality* of Christ's incarnation and the *proper interpretation* of Jesus' nature and personhood.

In this light, it may be necessary to revise traditional views about John's sacramental realism. For rather understandable reasons, Catholic exegetes have been historically inclined to treat the fourth gospel as the New Testament's sacramentary. Thus, John 6:51–59 is read with an emphasis on the *physical objects* mentioned there: bread, flesh, blood, food, drink. But recent scholarship has shown that, if we consider John's larger theological program in this passage, our customary emphasis may be misplaced. (See Cosgrove 1989, 522–39.) John's own concern in chapter 6 seems to be not objects but actions. The *verbs*—eating, drinking—form the center of his argument. Thus the literalism that John appears to encourage in this chapter focuses not on the recognition of bread as Christ's flesh but on the need for literal engagement in the actions of eating and drinking. The core of his argument is not "this bread is Christ's flesh" but rather "you must participate in the community's eucharistic meal by actually eating and drinking if you hope to receive the life of the risen Jesus." In a word, John's theological concern is the meaning of the *actions,* not the meaning of the elements. Charles Cosgrove has summarized this point well:

> [T]he point of the *literal* eating and drinking in John 6:53ff. lies in the fact that participation in the eucharistic meal represents public identification with the Johannine community as an indispensable condition for "abiding in Jesus" and thus receiving his Life. For the risen Jesus is present only in the community; in fact, his presence takes the form of "oneness" with [this] community (John 17). This does not mean that "the flesh" itself has the power to bestow life—whether the flesh of the elements or the flesh of the gathered community. It is the Spirit that gives life: the Spirit-Paraclete of the glorified Jesus present in the community *and nowhere else.* (529)

In sum, what eucharistic eating and drinking signifies is participation in the Johannine community. Such participation, of course, involves real risks. "It entails the risk of participation in Jesus' death, which eating Jesus' flesh and drinking his blood also signifies. Yet life is found nowhere else, because the living Jesus is present nowhere else than in the community of his disciples" (530). Cosgrove goes on to note that John's purpose in chapter 6:51–59 was primarily polemical, although the polemic is directed not so much against Jews as against "wannabe" disciples—"secret believers who have faith in Jesus but refuse to identify themselves with the Johannine community" (529)—in other words, people like Nicodemus. Although Nicodemus believes in Jesus and knows he comes from God, such faith *by itself* "does not pass the Johannine test for genuineness."

As Professor Wayne Meeks puts it, "[M]ere belief without joining the Johannine community, without making the decisive break with 'the world' . . . is a diabolic 'lie'" (Meeks 1972, 69). In sum, one must be "born again" of water and the Spirit in order to qualify for entry into the kingdom of God (as John insisted in 3:5). To put it another way, one must experience the *literal, public, visible, ecclesial* rite of baptism. The "life of the Spirit is present nowhere else but in the concrete fleshly existence of the community that bears the stigma and destiny of the Stranger from above" (Cosgrove 1989, 535). One must therefore walk the walk and not merely talk the talk, even if that means risking rejection, suffering and death. John is well aware that public confession of Jesus might result in either social death—excommunication from the Jewish community—or physical death (532).

John's sacramentalism might thus be interpreted as an early Christian version of *"extra ecclesiam nulla salus."* (This slogan goes back to Cyprian, Letter 73.21; see Cosgrove 1989, 535.) The difference is that by the third century, Cyprian was concerned to connect ortho*doxy* and life, while John is concerned to link that life with ortho*praxy* (536). For John, life is visible and present as love, as a crucified *love* alive in the church because of the presence of that "other Paraclete" whom Jesus promised to send, the Spirit. "'Life' is [thus] the place where Jesus is, and that place is the community of his followers who keep his word and love one another even unto death" (536).

Such life and love cannot be kept secret or hidden. They must become incarnate, public, visible, literal, real. They must be enacted in *real* deeds of initiatory washing, of eucharistic eating and drinking. A faith like Nicodemus's profits nothing. Note the sarcastic commentary about Nicodemus in John's account of Jesus' burial (John 19:39–42). In order to embalm Jesus' body, Nicodemus brings "about a hundred pounds" of aromatic spices and ointments—a hundred pounds! Obviously, Nicodemus did not *truly* understand who Jesus was as "the one who descended from heaven" (John 3:13), the preexistent Logos. He thought the Lord was going to have a long tenure in the grave. (See Cosgrove 1989, 537–38). John's point is clear and sharp: Those who refuse to follow Jesus to the *place* where he is cannot recognize who Jesus is. In the fourth gospel, life is a closed circle:

> The statements alluding to baptism and the eucharist in John specify certain conditions for participation in this circle. . . . In the Fourth Gospel obedience is the prerequisite for seeing (14:21), which is the prerequisite for believing (20:8; 20:31), which is the prerequisite for obedience (16:1; 6:60–65). This circle remains unbroken, and it encloses the place where eating the flesh of the Son of Man and drinking his blood means following him obediently to the place *in the world* where he is, to behold his glory. That place is the community with whom Jesus and the Father are united through the Spirit-Paraclete, the community of those who share the Son of Man's alienation from the world, the community of Jesus' friends who love one another even unto death. (539)

Like Paul, therefore, John's gospel was concerned to explain how Christians come to participate in Jesus Christ and the life he offers. John's explanation was emphatically ecclesiological and pneumatological. (It might be noted that, as Raymond Brown and other scholars have shown, John's ecclesiology had strongly sectarian overtones that we might not find acceptable today.) It was John's sacramentalism (and its deutero-Pauline parallels in literature like Ephesians and Titus) that eventually triumphed within the Catholic tradition.

5.   *Post–New Testament sacramentalism.* It is clear, however, that even at the end of the New Testament era there were profound disagreements among Christians over the meaning of sacramental rites

like baptism and eucharist. A revealing case is found in the *Didache,* an early Christian "church order" that scholars today believe probably developed alongside Matthew's gospel in the church of Antioch (the first truly interracial Christian community, the church that helped Paul launch his missionary career). The *Didache* very likely represents the concerns of more conservative Jewish Christians who still believed in the validity and importance of Torah observance (as interpreted through Christian *halakah* or "oral tradition"). These conservatives were deeply troubled—indeed, scandalized—by the practice of free and easy table-fellowship between Gentiles and Jews. They saw missionaries like Paul as traitors who had betrayed their own roots, their own people. These same conservatives were ready to preach what Jesus preached, but they were not quite ready to preach Jesus.

Thus, when one reads the brief account of baptism in *Didache* 7, one finds none of Paul's "death and burial with Christ" ideology. For the community of the *Didache,* baptism does not plunge the believer into Jesus' death, nor does it unite the believer to the body of Christ, nor does it create a community of equals. (See Galatians 3:28.) Jews, as God's elect and chosen people, are still superior to Gentile converts. Gentiles are clearly second-class citizens who are expected ultimately to take on full Torah observance. (Thus the *Didache* rejects Paul's view and insists that one must become a Jew first in order to become a Christian).

In a word, the *Didache* sees sacraments—baptism, the eucharistic meal—as having an *eschatological* content but not necessarily a *christological* content. The *Didache* never cites the tradition, quoted by Paul in 1 Corinthians 11, about Jesus' deeds at table "on the night when he was betrayed." Nor do the eucharistic prayers of the *Didache* identify the elements of bread and wine with Jesus' body and blood. This means that through baptism and eucharist Christians are joined not necessarily to Christ (as Paul or John would have it) but rather are joined to the eschatological age, the era in which an utterly new relationship between God and humankind has arrived in the world through the resurrection of Jesus. Resurrection is thus not a statement about Jesus' body but an affirmation that the eschatological era has arrived and is now available to all who believe as Jesus did.

Luke as a Eucharistic Gospel

Finally, I want to call attention to recent work on the gospel of Luke. As New Testament scholar S. S. Bartchy has written:

> One distinctive feature of Jesus' ministry was his practice of a radically inclusive and non-hierarchical table fellowship as a central strategy in his announcement and redefinition of the inbreaking rule of God. In so doing, Jesus challenged the inherent exclusivism and status consciousness of accepted social and religious custom and presented a living parable of a renewed Israel. (Bartchy 1992, 796)

Bartchy's point echoes the comments made a generation earlier by the renowned British Baptist scholar Norman Perrin, who wrote:

> The "table-fellowship of the Kingdom" . . . was a feature of the common life of Jesus and his followers . . . and a symbol of the new kind of relationship made possible by the common acceptance of the challenge. Scribe, tax collector, fisherman and Zealot came together around the table at which they celebrated the joy of the present experience and anticipated its consummation in the future.
>
> The central feature of the message of Jesus is, then, the challenge of the forgiveness of sins and the offer of the possibility of a new kind of relationship with God and with one's fellow [men and women]. This was symbolized by a table-fellowship . . . of such joy and gladness that it survived the crucifixion and provided the focal point for the community life of the earliest Christians, and was the most direct link between that community life and the pre-Easter fellowship of Jesus and his disciples. (Perrin 1967, 107)

In Luke's gospel, especially, Jesus always seems to be either *at table* or *on his way to or from a meal*. Even after Easter, on the road to Emmaus, Jesus the stranger meets disappointed disciples and breaks bread with them, opening their hearts and eyes to his risen presence. Indeed, Luke's special name for the eucharist—*he klasis tou artou,* "the breaking of bread"—appears in both the gospel (24:53) and the book of Acts (2:42). The oldest name for eucharist in the New Testament is not Luke's, however, but the phrase found in Paul's first letter to the Corinthians (11:20–21), *to kyriakon deipnon,* "the Lord's Supper." The word "eucharist" itself, as a noun, never appears in the New Testament, although the verb *eucharistein* appears fairly often and early. It is found already in the passage from 1 Corinthians 11:23–25 just alluded to.

Searching for the Origins of Christian Eucharist

Before we look in greater detail at Jesus' meals and table-ministry in Luke, some comments are in order about how scholars today view the origins of Christian eucharist.

1.   Eugene LaVerdiere has written, "The origin of the Eucharist is inseparable from Jesus' passion and resurrection. The Eucharist pre-supposes that Jesus gave his life for others. . . . From the point of view of the Eucharist, what is significant is not simply the fact that Jesus suffered and died, but that he suffered *for others* and gave his life *that all might live*" (LaVerdiere 1996, 3, emphasis added).

LaVerdiere's remarks make two points clear: First, that we must look for the origins of eucharist in the paschal mystery of Jesus rather than in some attempted historical reconstruction of his life and ministry. Whatever we may conclude about Jesus' own historical meal-practice and table ministry, it was in light of their community experience of access to the Risen One that Christians celebrated *he kyriakon deipnon* (the Lord's Supper) and *he klasis tou artou* (the breaking of bread). In other words, when the earliest Christians cele-brated eucharist, they were not necessarily trying to imitate in some direct or literal manner Jesus' own deeds at table. Jesus' own histor-ical practice should probably be thought of as tablature, as a kind of musical score aimed at performance (his own and that of others to come after him). Christian eucharist was a rereading, a retelling, a redefining—in short, a *performance*—of the "score" Jesus created in his dealings with others at table.

The second point flows from Jesus' self-surrender, his sacrifice *for others,* his life given *that people might live.* The ultimate meaning of sacrifice—in the cross and resurrection of Jesus—is not the vio-lent, bloody destruction of a victim but a life freely given to and for others. This point is crucial because many Catholics believe that "to offer sacrifice" means to deny, demolish, devastate and destroy, that the core of sacrifice is suffering and destruction, a "giving up." But Christian tradition insists that by his suffering and death Jesus freely and fully *surrendered* his life. Jesus' life wasn't stolen or seized or violently wrested away from an unwilling victim. Even Mark's Jesus— anguished and troubled, distressed and pushed to the bitterest brink as he cries out "My God, my God, why have you forsaken me?"— breathes his last in such a way that the Roman centurion at the foot of the cross remarks, "Truly this man was the Son of God!" (Mark 14:33; 15:34, 39). Take away surrender and there is no sacrifice, at least as Christians understand the term. Seen from this angle, murder—like grand larceny—isn't a sacrifice at all; it's a vicious, terrible crime. Thomas Aquinas affirms this point, incidentally, when he writes, *"Illi qui Christum occiderunt, non fecerunt aliquod sacrum, sed magnam malitiam perpetraverunt. Ergo passio Christi potius fuit maleficium quam sacrificium"*; "Those responsible for slaying Christ did not perform a sacred action; rather, they committed great malice. [Seen from this angle], therefore, the passion of Christ was not a sacrifice but a crime" (*Summa Theologiae*, IIIa.48.3, *obj.* 3).

In the Latin theological tradition (represented by theologians like Augustine and Aquinas), the meaning of sacrifice lies not in immolation (the slaying of victims, their violent destruction) but in the precincts of the human heart—the deep core, the inner attitude or outlook—of the one offering. As Augustine formulates it, *"Sacrificium visibile, invisibilis sacrificii sacramentum, id est, sacrum signum est"* ("A *visible* sacrifice is a sacrament—or sacred sign—of an *invisible* sacrifice" [*De civitate dei*, Book X, c. 5]). Augustine then quotes Psalm 51: 18–19: "When I offer a holocaust, the gift does not please you; so I offer my shattered spirit, a changed heart you welcome." And he offers this commentary: "Notice how the prophet, by saying that God does *not* want sacrifice, shows that God *does* want it." But what God wants *isn't* "a slaughtered animal; it's . . . a shattered, surrendering heart." (See *De civitate dei*, Book X, c. 5.) Thus, during the passion, it was not Jesus' executioners who offered sacrifice but *Jesus himself*. Ultimately, the meaning of Jesus' sacrifice was located not in his suffering body but in his willing heart. And this is precisely the reason why LaVerdiere can write:

> The Eucharist presupposes that Jesus *offered* his life in the passion-resurrection. Its beginnings coincide with the experience of Jesus *continuing to offer* his life as risen Lord. The Eucharist is inseparable from Jesus' passion, death and resurrection. (LaVerdiere 1996, 3, emphasis added)

2.   A second point about searching for the origins of Christian eucharist follows from the first: In the New Testament, the Greek word that connects Jesus with the eucharist of Christians is the verb *ophthe* (grammatically, an aorist passive, third person singular; from the verb *horao,* to see). *Ophthe* is usually translated "he (Jesus) *appeared*," as in joyful cry the concludes the Emmaus story in Luke 24:34: "The Lord has truly been raised and *has appeared* (Greek, *ophthe*) to Simon!" It is the word that the New Testament writers often used to explain how Jesus, the Risen One, made himself known to the disciples after Easter. And although the common English translation is "he appeared," it would be probably be more accurate to say Jesus "made himself seen." This makes awkward English, but it better captures the nuances of the Greek.

What the word *ophthe* tries to convey is how Christians gained access to the Risen One on this side of Easter. That, after all, was the great crisis, the challenge, the question that Easter raised. We forget sometimes that Easter was a question, not an answer, that the tomb's emptiness was a source of trembling and terror, as we discover from reading Mark 16:8. If Jesus is dead, he belongs to the past and is inaccessible. But if Jesus has made himself seen, then what? What if Jesus is now making himself available to human sight and sensation, to human experience? What if the bread-breaker is making himself known in the breaking of bread, in *he klasis tou artou,* in the community's bread broken and shared? Then what? The Greek word *ophthe* suggests that at the origins of eucharist, two realities are at work: *God's initiative* on the one hand and *human hunger* on the other. Jesus made himself seen to disciples (God's initiative)—and this seeing took place in the context of a *community meal* (where human hungers—for food, for fellowship—are satisfied). Marianne Sawicki summarizes all this quite succinctly in her book *Seeing the Lord:*

> The Gospels identify Jesus with needy little ones. To see or recognize the Risen Lord is to see him in them. To reach them is to reach him. But the Gospels also inquire into the dynamics of recognizing Jesus mystically, spiritually present during worship. These two possible modes of Jesus' availability, through care and through cult, mutually support each other and are secured in each other. (Sawicki 1994, 334)

Care and cult become the two modes by which the risen presence of Jesus is known and named. Ordinarily, as Sawicki points out, people use social class and rank to "negotiate and struggle" to get "access to the economic food chain" (291). But the gospels claim that Jesus' teaching subverted that struggle based on status, social standing, class and rank. Jesus proposed something revolutionary:

> Hunger is now designated as the baseline competence for hearing God's word and for access to the Risen Lord. You [can] "see him" only by coming into contact with hunger: by being hungry and by feeding the hungry. You [can] "enter the kingdom" only if you root and snuffle around for it like a hungry infant wanting to nurse. God's kingdom [is] imaged as the table where there are places for everyone, and everyone has the place of honor, and everyone gets enough. The only table like that is [a mother's] breast, the table where someone smiles and says, Eat my body, and where the little child has the place of honor forever. (291)

As Eugene LaVerdiere summarizes it,

> The beginnings of the Eucharist were both simple and awesome. They were simple in that the community of disciples were ordinary men and women who gathered for an ordinary meal. They were awesome in that the personal presence and appearance of Christ transformed the community of disciples into a new people, men and women who shared in the risen life of Christ and transformed their meal into what would eventually be called, "The Lord's Supper." . . .
> Above all, what distinguished [the Christian meal] was the presence and experience of the risen Lord among them, filling

those who had suffered so much grief with a joy they had never known. Luke gives an inkling of this joy in the words of the disciples of Emmaus after they recognized the risen Lord: "Were not our hearts burning [within us] while he spoke to us on the way and opened the scriptures to us?" (LaVerdiere 1996, 5, 8)

Feasting with Jesus in the Kingdom of God

One of the striking things about the gospel of Luke (and one of the characteristics that distinguishes him from the other evangelists) is, therefore, an exquisite attention to the *table*. For Luke, table is the site of recognition where Jesus is "known in the breaking of bread"; the place where people gather in freedom, fear and hope; the "breast of God where even little children may rest their heads"; the place where "instruction flows sweet as kisses and clean as tears"; the "home of the homeless, the larder of the poor." (See Sawicki 1994, 296–97.) Luke tells the story of Jesus' mission as a prophet (in Galilee and, later, in Jerusalem) by telling the story of Jesus, the *bread-breaker* who becomes the *bread broken*. Jesus' history—and that of his disciples—thus becomes a history of food, a history of *table-fellowship*. Jesus' life is portrayed as

> one great journey in which meals and simple hospitality play a critical part for him as well as for his followers. Jesus, his disciples, all who would follow later, and the church itself are a people on a journey, a people of hospitality, both offered and received. The eucharist is the supreme expression of this hospitality, sustaining them on their journey to the kingdom of God. (LaVerdiere 1994, 9)

It is fair, on these terms, to imagine Luke as a table-centered gospel, a eucharistic gospel, a gospel of hospitality.

There can be little doubt that in Luke's narrative, table-fellowship constitutes a consistent and powerful literary motif. The third gospel contains no less than ten stories of Jesus at table with disciples and others. (See LaVerdiere 1996, 11, note 13. The passages are: [1] 5:27–39; [2] 7:36–50; [3] 9:10–17; [4] 10:38–42; [5] 11:37–54; [6] 14:1–24; [7] 19:1–10; [8] 22:14–38; [9] 24:13–35; [10] 24:36–53.)

There are several ways one could group these stories. In his book *Dining in the Kingdom of God*, LaVerdiere proposes four groupings:

1.   *At Table with Jesus the Prophet* in his Galilean ministry (#1–3)

2.   *At Table with Jesus the Prophet* on his way to Jerusalem (#4–7)

3.   *At Table with Jesus the Christ* at the celebration of Passover (#8, the "Last Supper"; Luke, incidentally, is the only synoptic writer who explicitly calls Jesus' farewell supper with his friends a Passover meal—although Mark and Matthew assume a Passover context)

4.   *At Table with Jesus the Lord* (#9–10, the risen Jesus' meal with the disappointed disciples on the road to Emmaus, and his meal with the community in Jerusalem)

Another New Testament scholar, Dennis Smith, suggests that we consider grouping Luke's table-stories according to their major themes (Smith 1987, 613–38). This arrangement helps to illustrate the connections between how Jesus *preaches* and how Jesus *practices*, between how Jesus becomes our food *on* the table and how Jesus forms and gathers a community *at* the table. The following is an outline of the four principal groups of Lukan table-stories as Smith analyzes them.

1.   The first group highlights what might be called "Jesus and the new ethics of the table." Here Luke's literary emphasis is upon the way Jesus critiqued common cultural practices of the ancient Mediterranean world. In the world where Jesus lived, one's status, rank and social position determined one's place at table. To understand this point, one must imagine a formal banquet at which only adult male guests recline on couches arranged in a "U" around the table, with their left elbows on the tabletop and their feet pointing away, toward the outside walls of the room. Women, slaves and children had to eat sitting; only free adult male citizens were permitted to recline. Ordinarily, a meal had two major parts: the *deipnon* (the vegetable, fish and, rarely, meat courses), followed by the *symposion* or

"cocktail party," where watered wine flowed freely and abundantly. (Note that the drinking party followed, rather than preceded, the meal.) Social standing was signified by the place offered to each guest by the host, as well as by the kind, amount and sequence of foods. Posture, position and food all served as codes that embodied—and enforced—a rather rigid pattern of social relationships. The table thus became a social map that revealed insiders and outsiders, haves and have-nots, superiors and inferiors, the powerful and the powerless.

Within such a cultural context, Jesus heralded a new and potentially explosive ethical principle; he announced a disturbing new way of evaluating and rewarding human behavior. The name of this new ethical principle (as Luke portrays it in chapter 14:7–11) is humility. Humility is a way of living with others based not on making comparisons between richer and poorer, greater and lesser, more important and less important. Jesus seems to have believed that the social climate and religious culture of his time and place promoted a pattern of human relationships based on violence, coercive power and competition—based on hoarding goods, having power and dominating or controlling others.

This pattern, Jesus insists in Luke, leads to rivalry, hatred, violence and despair. The solution lies in voluntary renunciation, humility, a complete conversion *based on a refusal to make comparisons.* "When you are invited [to a banquet]," Luke has Jesus saying, "go and recline in the lowest place, so that when your host comes he may say to you, 'Friend, go up higher.' . . . For if you exalt yourself you will be humbled, and if you humble yourself you will be exalted'" (Luke 14:10–11). Jesus then goes on to say that if you hold a lunch or a dinner, don't invite people who can repay you; instead, he says to "invite the poor, the crippled, the lame, the blind; blessed indeed will you be because of their inability to repay you" (Luke 14:13).

So the new ethical principle for table-companionship that Jesus announces is the *inability* to repay, the *refusal* to make comparisons, the radical *rejection* of all those violent, competitive, coercive, power-driven strategies that cause people to look out for number one. In Luke 14, Jesus suggests that all our social maps need to be redrawn, starting with seating arrangements at table.

2. The second set of Lukan stories highlights "Jesus as one who teaches at table." The section above comments on Luke 14. The first verse of this chapter tells us that Jesus had gone "on a sabbath" to "dine at the home of one of the leading Pharisees." There follows a description of Jesus healing a man with dropsy, as well as two parables: one that includes Jesus' remarks about inviting people unable to repay (the poor, the crippled, the lame, the blind), and another that tells the tale of a great feast ("What if you gave a party and nobody came?"). Dennis Smith notes that Luke 14 is "a highly structured literary unit" that functions in much the same way that Plato's classical dialogue *The Symposium* does. Like Socrates in Plato's classic, Jesus here uses the table as a venue for teaching something new (and potentially scandalous) about who will feast in the kingdom of God. Specifically, Luke 14 highlights the theme of conflict between Jesus and the Pharisees. As Smith observes,

> The chapter begins with a sabbath controversy (14:1–6). Then it moves to a contrast between the pride of the Pharisees and the humility of Jesus (14:7–11). Next is the contrast between the community of the Pharisees and the community of Jesus (14:12–14; cf. 15:1–2). Then there is a contrast between the invited and the uninvited (14:15–24 [the parable of the "great feast"]). (Smith 1987, 622)

This pattern of "Jesus as one who teaches at table" is repeated often throughout Luke's gospel. An especially vivid example occurs in chapter 7, where Jesus contrasts the exuberant love and generous hospitality of the "sinful woman" with Simon the Pharisee's mean-spirited stinginess. Another famous example occurs in chapter 10 (the story of Martha and Mary), where Jesus teaches that anxiety and worry are futile, arguing that only one thing is needed. And perhaps the most memorable picture of Jesus teaching at table is the Last Supper (Luke 22:14–38). There, Jesus conducts a mini-seminar that recapitulates themes from his entire ministry: the blessings of powerlessness; the supreme importance of humble service; the need for reliance upon God's gracious providence; the great reversal that awaits those who think they hold power and dominion over others.

3.   The third set of Lukan stories highlights the "table as a symbol of luxury." Such luxury, Jesus' teaching suggests, is both positive and negative, both blessing and curse.

In order to understand how Jesus used the table as a bipolar symbol of luxury, we need to recall that in the ancient Mediterranean world, the table was often the site for luxurious display. Upper-class images and ideologies colored cultural perceptions of what goes on (or should go on) when people dine together. Thus, for example, reclining at table promoted a ritzy aura of royal privilege; the posture itself pointed to the power and pleasures enjoyed by the idle rich. In the homes of the wealthy, the furniture, fabrics and accoutrements of the dining room spoke a language of ease and comfort, of silky softness, of seductive music and entertainment. And in fact, during the symposium or drinking party portion of a classical banquet, a flute-girl was often invited into the dining room after the tables were cleared. In Israel's prophetic tradition, these luxurious table arrangements were often the object of anger, scorn, sarcasm and ridicule. The diatribe of the prophet Amos (6:4–7) is justly famous:

> Woe to those who lie upon beds of ivory,
> and stretch themselves upon their couches,
> and eat lambs from the flock, . . .
> who sing idle songs to the sound of the harp, . . .
> who drink wine in bowls,
> and anoint themselves with the finest oils,
> but are not at all grieved over the ruin of Joseph!

One can almost hear the cat-like purring, feel the sinuous stretching of these spoiled rich folk in Amos's bitter words. Jesus, too, as Luke presents him (to a largely Gentile audience), belongs to this critical prophetic tradition. Like Amos, Jesus suggests that the luxurious meals of the heartless and self-absorbed rich are "a symbol for the debauchery of 'this age,'" which will be "condemned in the future judgment" (Smith 1987, 624). Thus, in Luke 12, Jesus tells the parable of that rich fool whose motto is "eat, drink and be merry" (Luke 12:16–21).

But perhaps a more stunning story is found in Luke 16:19–31, in the parable of "Dives (the Rich Man) and Lazarus." In this story, the table as a *negative* symbol of luxury is described with a vengeance. As Jesus tells the tale, the heartlessness of Dives looms large; his cruelty is gargantuan, boundless. Lazarus, a poor man covered with so many sores that the dogs come and lick him, "longs for even a scrap falling from the table." Both men die, and a great reversal occurs. Lazarus lands in the bosom of Abraham, while Dives rots in the lowest circle of hell, where he is tortured by thirst and the flames. The conclusion of Luke's story is especially chilling. When Dives asks Abraham to send messengers to warn his brothers of their impending doom, Abraham replies, "Forget it. They wouldn't be persuaded even if someone were to rise from the dead!"

Jesus was not, of course, a teacher whose focus was primarily negative. It will thus not surprise us to learn that Luke presents the Last Supper as a *positive* luxury meal. Jesus tells his friends how eagerly he longs "to eat this Passover" with them. Then he presides at a joyous feast that *anticipates* the messianic new age and *symbolizes* what is meant by dining in the kingdom of God.

Notice how different Luke's version of the Last Supper is from Mark's. As has been noted earlier in this essay, Mark sees Jesus' farewell meal as still another wearisome example of how stupid and thickheaded the apostles are. But in contrast, Luke views Jesus' final meal as a foretaste of that future table where every tear will be wiped away, where all suffering will cease, and where God and humankind will sit together in peace and fulfillment, eating and drinking in the kingdom of God. In this way, of course, Luke sets up the conditions for Christian eucharist, where Jesus' presence to the community "becomes focused on the meal. Whenever the presence of the risen Lord is . . . experienced in the church, it is . . . associated especially with the communal meal" (Smith 1987, 629).

4.   The fourth and final set of Lukan stories highlights "table as a symbol for community service and community fellowship." Scholars today generally agree that Jesus used the table not only to announce the in-breaking of God's reign into the human world—the arrival of God's presence and power here and now—but also to announce what kind of future awaits humankind. That future, Jesus proclaimed, is blessing, bounty, abundance, joy, gratitude—a festive

future where every human hunger will be satisfied and every tear wiped away. That blessed future, that new creation, is not so much a place but a *person*—the person of Jesus himself and the persons who are his body (believers, the church), for Jesus rises not only as bread but as a *people*. Of this "present-future," of this new creation, the table is Jesus' chosen ritual symbol. As Dennis Smith writes, "The joys of the end [time] are [already] realized in table fellowship with Jesus now; his ministry offers bread to the hungry, just as his table fellowship offers forgiveness to the penitent" (Smith 1987, 633). The future that Jesus promises is a future we are urged to share with the poor, the marginalized, the outcast, for perhaps the central theme of Luke's theology is

> that salvation has come to the "poor," a term that is given symbolic reference to the idea of social outcasts in general. A primary means whereby Luke presents this theme is the image of table fellowship, for it is characteristic of Jesus' ministry that "he eats with tax collectors and sinners" . . .
> In Luke Jesus' entire ministry is characterized as [a ministry] to the poor, the captives, the blind, the oppressed (Luke 4:18–19; see also 6:20–26, 7:22, 14:15–24, etc.). . . .
> The symbolic references to outcasts are expanded to include not only the poor but also the blind, the lame, the lepers, the deaf, etc. [in other words all those categories of "disabled" people whom society is often inclined to ignore, neglect, hide and even punish]. [Thus] . . . Jesus' table companions at the messianic banquet are defined as "the poor and maimed and blind and lame" (14:21). (636–37)

As Christian disciples, our future is to dine in the kingdom of God surrounded not by the powerful rich but *by those from whom we have most to learn:* sinners, the poor, the disabled, the sick, the unclean, the outcast. For it is to such as these that God's kingdom—that God's own self—belongs. That is the profoundly disturbing, revolutionary message of Jesus.

Some Conclusions about Jesus' Table Teaching in Luke

We are now in a position to draw some conclusions based on the research of scholars such as S. S. Bartchy, Eugene LaVerdiere and Dennis Smith.

1.   As S. S. Bartchy observes, "Luke gives more attention to table etiquette, table fellowship and the households in which these meals were eaten than any other New Testament writer. He highlights hospitality and food-sharing as occasions which display the sharp contrast between the radical inclusiveness of Jesus' mission and the various degrees of exclusiveness demanded by his competitors for renewing Israel, the Pharisees and scribes, who repeatedly charged Jesus with 'receiving sinners and eating with them'" (Bartchy 1992, 798).

2.   A unique feature of Luke is his presentation of Jesus as *a teacher at table*. Luke tends to present Jesus as a witty, urbane philosopher who is very much in his element at the symposium which, we saw, was the technical term for the second part of a formal banquet—the cocktails and conversation part, the entertainment that followed the food. Luke thus employs a classical Greco-Roman literary theme that his *Gentile* Christians could understand, even though they lacked the *Jewish* experience of ritual meals and symbolic foods. Luke uses this meal model as a means of highlighting Jesus' rather radical views on important matters like purity regulations, social boundaries, belonging, inclusion versus exclusion, and so on (798–99).

3.   Bartchy points out that Luke's emphasis on Jesus' inclusivity, his violation of purity laws, his willingness to eat with "immoral" types, would have been "hard bread" not only for devout Pharisaic Jews but also for elite and wealthy Christians. "For participation in such a socially inclusive community," Bartchy observes, "might well have cut them off from their prior social networks on which their status depended. From the perspective of Luke and Acts together, God intends this new community to offer reconciliation and solidarity among Jews and Gentiles, men and women, rich and poor" (799).

4.   The accusation repeated a number of times in Luke—that Jesus befriended tax collectors—is an especially telling point. These people were often frauds and shysters, flimflam artists who "were shunned by most people not so much because of their ritual impurity as because of their reputation for dishonest gouging of both rich and poor" (797). There is thus good reason to believe that Jesus did, in fact, associate frequently—at table and elsewhere—with persons widely viewed as disreputable and immoral.

> And as one who claimed to speak for God, his indiscriminate behavior greatly offended a wide spectrum of people who had been injured by the likes of Levi. In his message and table praxis, eating with anyone who would eat with him, Jesus challenged the central role played by table fellowship in reinforcing boundaries and statuses widely believed to be sanctioned by God. His use of table fellowship as a divine tool for undermining boundaries and hierarchies made him an enemy of social stability in the eyes of leading contemporaries. (797)

5.   We may thus conclude by saying that in Luke's eucharistic gospel, Jesus is presented as a living parable of how a renewed Israel—indeed, of how a renewed human community—might "live together from God's abundance" (799). God's rule ("kingdom") is imagined as food and drink, and "home" is presented as "a roving banquet hall" where even God seeks companions. At God's table, people are offered freedom and reconciliation, "a true home . . . spiritual and material abundance, as the basis for offering all these good things to each other, to others yet to come, and even to enemies" (800). As Jesus says in Luke 13:29, "People will come from the east and the west, from the north and the south, and will recline at table in the kingdom of God."

Summary

The New Testament period does not provide us with a uniform record about the significance of sacraments generally or about eucharist specifically. Mark saw the key to understanding Jesus' eucharistic teaching in his miraculous feeding of the multitudes, in his superabundant response to human hunger and need. Paul and John clearly affirmed that the Christian participates in Christ (though they differed on precisely how this happens). They clearly saw baptism and eucharist as essential to the identity, belief and praxis of Christians. But in a sense, their view is the reverse of ours. Our concern is: How does *Christ* become present in these sacraments, in this baptismal bath, in these elements of bread and wine? Their question was: How do *believers* become present to the mystery of Christ alive— through grace, faith and the Spirit—in the church? How does the Spirit-Paraclete bring believers into contact with the life that is Jesus? How does Jesus' table teaching and ministry continue in the eucharistic activity of Christians?

References to Works Cited in the Text

Bartchy, S. S. 1992. "Table Fellowship," in *Dictionary of Jesus and the Gospels,* edited by Joel B. Green and Scot McKnight. Downers Grove, Illinois: InterVarsity Press.

Cosgrove, Charles H. 1989. "The Place Where Jesus Is: Allusions to Baptism and the Eucharist in the Fourth Gospel." *New Testament Studies* 522–39.

Crossan, John. 1991. *The Historical Jesus.* San Francisco: Harper.

Keck, Leander. 1979. *Paul and His Letters.* Philadelphia: Fortress Press.

Klosinski, Edward. 1988. "The Meals in Mark" (doctoral dissertation).

LaVerdiere, Eugene. 1994. *Dining in the Kingdom of God.* Chicago: Liturgy Training Publications.

———. 1996. *The Eucharist in the New Testament and the Early Church.* Collegeville: The Liturgical Press/Pueblo.

Meeks, Wayne. 1972. "The Man from Heaven and Johannine Sectarianism." *Journal of Biblical Literature* 91: 44–72.

Meier, John. 1991. *A Marginal Jew: Rethinking the Historical Jesus,* vol. 1, *Roots of the Problem and the Person.* New York: Doubleday.

———. 1994. *A Marginal Jew: Rethinking the Historical Jesus,* vol. 2, *Mentor, Message, and Miracles.* New York: Doubleday.

O'Collins, Gerald. 1994. "What Are They Saying about Jesus Now?" *America* 171 (27 August–3 September 1994): 10–14, 32–35.

Perrin, Norman. 1967. *Rediscovering the Teaching of Jesus*. New York: Harper and Row.

Pontifical Biblical Commission (PBC). 1994. "The Interpretation of the Bible in the Church." *Origins* 23:497, 499–524.

Sawicki, Marianne. 1994. *Seeing the Lord*. Minneapolis: Fortress.

Schillebeeckx, Edward. 1979. *Jesus*, translated by Hubert Hoskins. New York: Seabury.

———. 1980. *Christ*, tranlated by John Bowden. New York: Seabury.

Schnackenburg, Rudolf. 1963. *God's Rule and Kingdom*, translated by John Murray. New York: Herder and Herder.

Sheehan, Thomas. 1988. *The First Coming*. New York: Random House Vintage.

Smith, Dennis. 1987. "Table Fellowship as a Literary Motif in the Gospel of Luke." *Journal of Biblical Literature* 106:613–38.

Thomas Aquinas. 1963. *Summa Theologiae*, vol. 58. Translated by William Barden. New York: McGraw-Hill.

Sacramental Presence: Contexts for the Contemporary Discussion

Real Presence as a Cultural Question

In his book *Real Presences*, Professor George Steiner describes a pre-occupation in modern culture with the question of transcendence (or divine presence). Steiner had explored aspects of this question in an earlier collection of essays entitled *Language and Silence*. Steiner contends that the problem of presence is not only a theological one but a cultural one as well. Traditional societies in the West, he argues, believed in a meaningful "covenant" between word and world. They were convinced that the coherent use of language to communicate meaning and feeling was underwritten by the assumption of God's presence. In particular, they were convinced that the experience of *esthetic meaning*—in literature, the arts and especially music—inferred the "necessary possibility of [God's] real presence." (See Steiner 1989, 3.) In short, wherever and whenever human beings experience meaning, they implicitly affirm the presence of Ultimate Meaning, of the Word, of God's own self.

For many people today, Steiner notes, "no plausible reflection or belief underwrites [God's] presence. Nor does any intelligible evidence" (3). Modern culture often likens God to events like sunrise and sunset. Ever since Copernicus, we have known that the sun does not really rise or set, yet these figures of speech continue to inhabit our grammar and haunt our imaginations. They are like ghosts in an attic. People continue to refer to them, even though nobody actually believes in them. That, Steiner observes, is how many modern people have come to think about God and God's presence. "Where God [still] clings to our culture, to our routines of discourse, [God] is a phantom of grammar, a fossil embedded in the childhood of rational speech" (3). In short, much of the contemporary world sees God's presence as a dinosaur, a fantasy, an archaic accident of language.

In *Real Presences,* however, Steiner challenges this view and outlines a reverse argument. His main thesis is best summarized in his own words:

> This essay . . . proposes that any coherent understanding of what language is and how language performs, that any coherent account of the capacity of human speech to communicate meaning and feeling is, in the final analysis, underwritten by the assumption of God's presence. I will put forward the argument that the experience of aesthetic meaning in particular, that of literature, of the arts, of musical form, infers the necessary possibility of this "real presence." The seeming paradox of a "necessary possibility" is, very precisely, that which the poem, the painting, the musical composition are at liberty to explore and to enact.
>
> This study will contend that the wager on the meaning of meaning, on the potential of insight and response when one human voice addresses another, when we come face to face with the text and work of art or music, which is to say when we encounter the other in its condition of freedom, is *a wager on transcendence.*
>
> This wager . . . predicates that presence of a realness, of a "substantiation" (the theological reach of this word is obvious) within language and form. It supposes a passage, beyond the fictive or the purely pragmatic, from meaning to meaningfulness. The conjecture is that "God" *is,* not because our grammar is outworn, but that grammar lives and generates worlds because there is the wager on God. (3–4, emphasis added)

Steiner argues, in other words, that our human ability to experience meaning in the arts (especially nonverbal arts like music) is predicated on the "necessary possibility" of God's presence, of transcendence. All art is a rendezvous with meaning, with intelligibility. Every work of art is an *opus metaphysicum*. Every creative act assumes that meaning is possible, plausible and palpable as a presence that exceeds the work itself. (See Steiner 1989, 134.) Indeed, Steiner claims, the whole of Western esthetics and epistemology (to say nothing of theology and metaphysics) has taken this concept of presence as axiomatic. Whether that presence is understood as God, as Plato's Ideas, as Descartes' self-consciousness, as Kant's transcendent logic, or as Heidegger's Being, it remains the *center* toward which all "the spokes of meaning finally lead." "That presence, theological, ontological or metaphysical, makes credible the assertion that there 'is something in what we say'" (121). For Steiner signs truly *signify;* references are *real;* words convey *presences.*

Steiner's position is, of course, congenial to traditional Roman Catholic sacramentalism, which is rooted in the notion that the relation between *signum* and *signatum* is a real one, that symbols disclose and embody the realities they symbolize. Similarly, Steiner argues that until quite recently we humans assumed there was a trustworthy covenant between word and world. Our interactions with one another were based on the conviction that there is a fiduciary contract between word and object, between signs and what they signify, between language and reality. We assumed that the world— that being itself—is "sayable," that reality and truth can be expressed, embodied and enacted through words. As Steiner notes:

> There would be no history as we know it, no religion, metaphysics, politics or aesthetics as we have lived them, without [this] initial act of trust [without the confidence that this world— and our lives in it—can really and truly be "put into words"]. Only in the light of that confiding can there be a history of meaning which is, by exact counterpart, a meaning of history. From Gilgamesh's song of mutinous sorrow over his fallen companion [Enkidu] . . . to the present, the relationship between word and world, inner and outer, has been held "in trust." That is to say that it has been conceived of and existentially enacted as a relation of responsibility. (89–90)

Indeed, the idea of human responsibility as a free moral act is rooted in this notion of semantic trust. For only if being is truly sayable, only if there is a real relationship between word and world, can we freely answer *to* and answer *for*. What is at stake here is not only meaning but ethics (responsibility), not only the destiny of human beings but the destiny of the divine. For from the outset, in the West, God's very self has been conceived as a speech-act, a Word, a call, a summons to answer and respond. "Western theology and the metaphysics, epistemology and aesthetics which have been its major footnotes, are 'logocentric,'" writes Steiner. "This is to say that they [take as axiomatic], as fundamental and pre-eminent, the concept of a 'presence'" (121). In a nutshell, meaning itself requires that we postulate the existence and presence of God. The axiom of meaning and the concept of God share the same origin. The conviction that being is sayable and the conviction that God exists "have the same place and time of birth" (119, citing Derrida).

An Outline of Steiner's Position

Steiner's argument can be summarized in this way:

1.   Human beings are precisely those creatures who have "broken free from the great silence of matter" (Steiner 1967, 36). Human consciousness has become matter's great poem. Language is thus the defining mystery of humankind, the mystery through which the identity and presence of the human become historically visible and explicit (x). We humans are possessed *of* speech and possessed *by* it. We are creatures defined by the word. We are animals in whom "the isolating privilege of speech" has become "definitional" (Steiner 1989, 89). In us, words choose the grossness and infirmity of flesh for their own compelling life. (See Steiner 1967, 36.) In us, being itself has acquired the ability to speak. All words thus have ontological roots, and so they are truly referential; they point beyond themselves to what is real and what really exists.

2.   Moreover, language—as we know, experience and use it—has boundless potential. "We can say any truth and any falsehood. We can affirm and negate in the same breath." All language, therefore,

"possesses and is possessed by the dynamics of fiction. To speak, either to oneself or to another, is in the most naked . . . sense . . . to invent, to re-invent being and the world" (Steiner 1989, 55). Language *creates*. Like Adam, it names all beings, forms and presences. Its adjectives qualify thoughts and deeds, thereby allowing us to conceptualize good and evil. Its predicates show us equations or subject objects to action. Its past tense allows us to reconstruct memory as history and hermeneutic. Most remarkable of all, our human languages have a future tense, a fact that is (as Steiner says) "a radiant scandal, a subversion of mortality . . . [for it makes] of the word a reaching out past death" (Steiner 1967, 38). Humans alone can "construct and parse the grammar of hope." We alone can say and unsay what exists and what does not. We can tell what the light is like in galaxies not yet discovered; we can describe the steady pulse of a universe still alive millennia after the sun has become a cold, dead star and our planet has disappeared.

3.   For humans, then, language offers a limitless field of possible meanings. Words are inexhaustible. "The chain of signs is infinite" (Steiner 1989, 59). "A sentence always means more" (82). There is no limit to the field of possible meanings that can occur when two liberties meet in a conversation, or when a text, moving across time and history, encounters an endless succession of readers.

4.   At the same time, however, language has limits, its frontiers. We arrive at situations in which words finally fail us, in spite of their exuberant fertility. That failure is an invitation to experience *transcendent* meaning and presence. As Steiner writes in a beautiful essay on "Silence and the Poet":

> It is decisively the fact that language does have its frontiers, that it borders on three other modes of statement—light, music, and silence—which gives proof of a transcendent presence in the fabric of the world. *It is just because we can go no further, because speech so marvelously fails us, that we experience the certitude of a divine meaning surpassing and enfolding ours.* What lies beyond [the human] word is eloquent of God. That is the joyously defeated recognition expressed in the poems of St. John of the Cross and of the mystic tradition.

Where the word of the poet ceases, a great light begins.
(Steiner 1967, 39, emphasis added)

5.　　Human history is thus *a history of meaning*. (See Steiner 1989, 89.) As Steiner says in an essay entitled "The Retreat from the Word," "We live inside the act of discourse" (Steiner 1967, 12). Western civilization is thus essentially verbal in character. It relies on the notion that words offer us access to reality, to truth and to meaning. It assumes (as philosophers like Thomas Aquinas did) that "words gather and engender responsible apprehensions of the truth" (20).

6.　　But with the emergence of modern mathematics, this verbal basis for Western life and thought—this trusted covenant between word and world—began to crumble. "The most decisive change in the tenor of Western intellectual life since the seventeenth century," writes Steiner, "is the submission of successively larger areas of knowledge to the modes and proceedings of mathematics" (15). After Descartes, the mathematician turned philosopher, the relationship between being and thought was reversed: *"Sum, ergo cogito"* became *"Cogito, ergo sum."* Implicitly, Cartesian philosophy identified truth with mathematical proof. In cardinal respects, *reality itself* was redefined. It now began *outside* verbal language, in the untranslatable world of a pure mathematics that no longer required a real relation between symbol and word. Truth became quantitative rather than qualitative, impersonal rather than personal, empirical rather than intuitive, mathematical rather than metaphysical. It was perceived, increasingly, as an abstract relation between numbers, rather than as a reality arrived at through referential signs. We could no longer trust the information coming to us through our senses. The sunrise was not really the sun rising. The huge steel girder was not really a solid mass, but a swirling dance of atomic and subatomic particles. The world itself thus became a kind of animate fiction.

7.　　Today therefore we have come face to face with the discomfiting implications of Gertrude Stein's witty sentence: "There is no there there." The contract between word and world has been nullified. Neither meaning nor presence are understood to arise from a real relation between word and object, sign and signified. In modern linguistic theory, signs are purely arbitrary. They are not like their objects; they do not express or embody realities. The fashionable literary theory known as deconstruction challenges the notion that words refer to some insured content or guaranteed meaning. Deconstructionists like Jacques Derrida thus argue that there are no fixed centers of meaning to which words provide access. We humans are not primarily *speaking* animals, we are *playing* animals. Words are not contracts that establish shared meanings and responsibilities; they are games. They point not to presence, but to absence. As Steiner summarizes it:

> [D]econstruction teaches us that where there is no "face of God" for the [word] to turn to, there can be no transcendent or decidable intelligibility. [To] break with the postulate of the sacred is [to] break with any stable, potentially ascertainable meaning of meaning. [When this happens, the notion of] a cognitively coherent and ethically responsible [self] is [also] dissolved. (Steiner 1967, 132)

It may well be that Steiner has overstated his case. Deconstructionists like Derrida may not be quite the demons he makes them out to be. Indeed, their work forces us to look straight at the emptiness, into the void, the unutterable loneliness of a language without fixed meanings and a world without a divine guarantor. Deconstruction forces us to come to terms with the fact that in the modern world God is often experienced not as a presence but as an absence.

We live on the other side of the Holocaust. We now know that people can read Goethe and Rilke in the evening, can play Bach and Schubert and Mozart, and then go to work at Auschwitz the next morning. (See Steiner 1967, ix.) Language—and the divine presence that insures its meaningfulness—have forever been altered by the systematic genocides of our century. As Steiner has observed, the greatest horrors of our century did not occur in silence. What happened was "recorded, catalogued, chronicled, set down" (99). Words that should never have entered a human mouth were, in fact, spoken. Words that should never have been set down on paper were, in fact, written:

Sacramental Presence

> In the Gestapo cellars, stenographers . . . took down carefully the noises of fear and agony wrenched, burned, or beaten out of the human voice. The tortures and experiments carried out on live beings at Belsen and Matthausen were exactly recorded. . . . When Polish rabbis were compelled to shovel out open latrines with their hands and mouths, there were German officers there to record the fact, to photograph it, and to label the photographs. (99–100)

In our time, the unspeakable has been spoken, the unthinkable has been written down, indexed and filed for future reference.

> Languages have great reserves of life. They can absorb masses of hysteria, illiteracy, and cheapness. . . . But there comes a breaking point. Use a language to conceive, organize, and justify Belsen; use it to make out specifications for gas ovens, use it to dehumanize [human beings] during twelve years of calculated bestiality. Something will happen to it. Make of words what Hitler and Goebbels and the hundred thousand *Untersturmführer* made: conveyors of terror and falsehood. Something will happen to the words. Something of the lies and sadism will settle in the marrow of the language. Imperceptibly at first, like the poisons of radiation sifting silently into the Body. The language will no longer grow and freshen. It will no longer perform, quite as well as it used to, its two principal functions: the conveyance of humane order which we call law, and the communication of the quick of the human spirit which we call grace. (101)

It is thus hardly surprising that Steiner sees in our century a broken covenant between word and world. The notion that "human meaning is underwritten by divine presence" went up in smoke in the ovens of Belsen and Auschwitz. Shortly before fleeing Nazi Germany, Thomas Mann wrote to the dean of the University of Bonn:

> The mystery of language is a great one; *the responsibility for a language . . . is of a symbolic and spiritual kind; this responsibility does not have merely an aesthetic sense.* The responsibility for language is, in essence, human responsibility. . . . Should a German writer, made responsible through his habitual use of language, remain silent, quite silent, in the face of all the irreparable evil which has been committed daily, and is being

committed [even now], against body, soul, and spirit, against justice and truth, against man and [woman]? (Cited in Steiner 1967, 102, emphasis added)

What Mann wrote of German must be said today of all human languages, for all are implicated in the guilty circle of silence that has characterized our epoch.

Summary

In classical Western culture, then, words were believed to disclose (to bestow) a meaning, an otherness beyond the limits of human discourse. This was precisely the linguistic basis for Aquinas's sacramental principle, *"Signa dantur hominibus, quorum est per nota ad ignota pervenire"* (*Summa Theologiae*, IIIa.60.2, *corpus*). Every sign, every symbol for Aquinas launches a search, a process of discovery through which we reconnect with something absent, something missing, something unknown, something transcendent. This, as Aquinas well knew, is the great paradox of symbols *(signa)*. While they embody (make present) what they symbolize, they can do this only if we agree, first, that there is something *absent* which needs to be made present. The symbol cannot lead us *"per nota ad ignota"* unless we first consent to an absence, a mysterious otherness, a reality deeper and greater than we are.

Thus, for Aquinas, every symbol constituted an invitation to self-transcendence. Moreover, every symbol embraced both *nota* and *ignota*. Or—to use the language of twentieth-century theology—every symbol exhibits a multivalent, dialectical character. This simply means that symbols are not flat, one-dimensional objects or reminders. They are, instead, transactions that disclose and embody relationships. Symbols simultaneously embrace many levels of human experience and discourse. They are never tidy or precise; they can never be tamed or domesticated; they are always messy, slightly out of focus and alive with ambiguity. Thus their paradoxical nature: They are visible, social and historical *(nota)* and at the same time hidden, mysterious, transcending time and space *(ignota)*.

The Catholic tradition has thus maintained (for nearly two millennia) that sacrament (*signum sacrum,* symbol) both comforts us

with presence and confronts us with an absence, an irreducible otherness, a mystery. And this relationship between comfort and con-
frontation, presence and absence, is a two-way street. It is not only
that the things known *(nota)* lead us to things unknown *(ignota)*, but
the reverse is true as well. In the eucharist, for instance, the known,
material quantities of bread and wine draw us into the mystery of
Christ's body and blood, but at the same time, the mystery of Christ's
body redefines matter and reconfigures perception. The reality of
sacrament forces us to recognize that matter itself must bear the
weight of spirit. If bread and wine can trigger access to a risen Body,
then the root of all matter has been transfigured.

Paradoxically, then, the path to presence leads through absence.
Upon encountering the unknown, we must completely redefine the
known. We discover what is immanent, what is closest to our hearts
and lives, only by accepting the otherness that enlivens every human
attempt to communicate meaning and feeling. That is the mystery
hidden in the depths of human language, just as it is the mystery that
underlies the Catholic tradition of sacrament. It may be argued, then,
that Catholic sacramentalism does depend, in a profound sense, upon
what Steiner calls the "covenant between word and world." It is
grounded upon the conviction that human history is a history of
meaning, and that today language must be recovered as revelation,
responsibility and grace.

In a word, the Catholic sacramental tradition operates on the
principle that we can encounter *God* fully only by encountering the
human fully. Human beings move *per nota ad ignota,* Aquinas says.
God's presence can be perceived only in human moments—moments
of wonder, beauty, goodness, grace and peace; moments of doubt and
fear; moments of limitation, loathing, loneliness and pain; moments
of resentment and anger. We arrive at mystery, at presence, at God,
only by arriving at the human with all its poignancy and terror.

The following section offers a short outline of some historical
principles that have accompanied the development of a distinctive,
Catholic notion of eucharistic real presence.

Eucharistic Presence: Outline of the Tradition

Principle 1: In Catholic tradition, sacramental presence is always an embodied presence, an incarnate presence.

When, in the eucharistic prayer, Christians call to mind the paschal mystery of Jesus, this remembering is not mere psychological recall. Rather, to remember or call to mind means to engage in an incarnate, corporate action. Sacramental memory, in the Catholic tradition, is a *deed,* not an idea; a *verb,* not a noun; an *action* and *outcome,* not an object.

1.   This principle is already adumbrated in John's gospel, with its emphasis on incarnate, public, literal, real eating and drinking as essential to participation in the Christian community. In John's view, one cannot participate in the life that is Jesus unless one participates in the rituals of the community that is gathered and active in the name of Jesus. (See the previous essay on "The Impact of Twentieth-Century Approaches to Scripture for Understanding the Connections between Jesus and Eucharist.")

2.   A similar line of thinking emerges in the sacramental theology of early Christian leaders like John Chrysostom. The following is a representative passage, taken from a homily on Matthew's gospel, that Chrysostom preached while still a presbyter at Antioch:

> The Word [of God] says, "This is my body"—let us reply "Amen!" Let us contemplate [this mystery] with the eyes of our spirit. For Christ did not give us just another fact to be recorded by the senses. Rather, [he revealed] that everything *grasped* by our senses can also be *understood* by our spirit. Take baptism, for instance. Water, the *material* element that bestows the gift, signifies a *spiritual* event—namely, [new] birth and renewal [of life]. If you had been [born] without a body, Christ could have given you bare, disembodied gifts. But because spirit and body are joined, *spiritual* gifts are given to you in *bodily* form. How many of you say, "I wish I could see Christ's form and figure, his clothing, his shoes!" Indeed! You do see him; you do touch him; you even eat him. And you want to see his clothes?! Really!

[Christ] has given you the ability not only to see him, but to eat and touch and take him within yourselves. . . .

Consider how great is the honor bestowed on you; consider how awesome is the table you enjoy. What even angels cannot see without trembling, what they dare not look upon because of its shimmering brightness—*that* we are fed by; *that* we are joined to, making us one body and one flesh with Christ. . . .

Through these mysteries, Christ joins himself to each one of the faithful. Those he begets [in baptism], he nourishes with his own bodily being . . . proving to you once more that he has taken on your very flesh. Since we have been counted worthy of so much love and honor, we should guard against growing blasé. Have you not ever noticed how eagerly a baby seizes its mother's breast, how ravenously it presses its lips onto the nipple? With the same eagerness, we ought to approach this table and the nipple of this spiritual cup. Or rather, with even greater enthusiasm, like babies at the breast, let us draw out the Spirit's grace. . . . The [mysteries] set before us are not derived from any human power. The one [Christ] who acted *then,* at *that* supper, acts *now* [at ours]. We occupy the place of servants; the one who sanctifies and transforms [the gifts] is [Christ] himself.

This table of ours is thus the same as his, and contains nothing less. . . . For Christ prepares *both* tables—his *and* ours. *This* table *is* that upper room, where [Jesus and his disciples] once gathered—and just as they left it to go to the Mount of Olives, so let us go out to [fill] the hands of the poor. For this place of ours, too, is the Mount of Olives, and the great multitude of the poor are olive trees planted in God's house-trees that yield for us a useful oil. For this is the oil the five [wise] virgins possessed. . . . Having received it, let us go in to meet the Bridegroom with lamps alight; then we may depart.

Let no one inhumane—no one cruel or merciless—approach [these holy mysteries]. (John Chrysostom, Sermon 82.4–5 on Matthew's gospel, author's translation)

One might note in passing that in this text, Chrysostom sees the significance of both Jesus' eucharistic body and the assembly's acts of eating and drinking in strongly feminine terms. The sacramental cup is a nipple; the people who drink from it are like babies hungrily seeking the mother's breast.

Principle 2: The mystery of matter reveals the mysteries of the spirit.

This second principle is the fundamental law of the whole Christian economy, a law enunciated in the fourth century by preachers like Chrysostom and reiterated in our own century by theologians like Karl Rahner, who argues that Christians are the world's "greatest materialists" because they believe that matter itself will be transfigured—indeed, *has already begun* to be transfigured—in the risen body of Jesus.

An illustration of this principle may be found in the old Latin preface for Christmas:

> *Quia per incarnati Verbi mysterium, nova mentis nostrae oculis lux tuae claritatis infulsit: ut dum visibiliter Deum cognoscimus, per hunc in invisibilium amorem rapiamur.* (Because through the mystery of the Word made flesh, the new light of your splendid beauty has shone upon the eyes of our mind: so that *knowing God visibly,* we might be snatched up into a love of things unseen.)

This visible knowing of God is a fleshly deed that involves a physically rooted recognition of God as *beauty,* as *splendor*—a knowledge of God who reveals and bestows the divine self through the worldly stuff of nature, history and humankind. The mystery of matter, the mystery of Christ enfleshed is the real presence, the real appearance of God's *amor invisibilis.*

As Hans Urs von Balthasar once noted, there is good reason why this ancient liturgical text used the word *amor* (that is, *eros*) to speak of God's love, rather than *caritas.*

> For what is at stake here is the movement effected by seeing what God has shown. This is a movement of the entire person, leading away from [the] self through the vision towards the invisible God, a movement . . . which the word "faith" describes only imperfectly, although it is in this movement that faith has its proper "setting in life" *(Sitz im Leben).* [This] transport of the soul . . . must . . . be understood in a strictly theological way. In other words, it must be understood not as a merely psychological response to something beautiful in a worldly sense which has been encountered through vision, but as the movement of

[our] whole being away from . . . self and towards God through Christ, a movement founded on the divine light of grace in the mystery of Christ. But the whole truth of this mystery is that the movement which God (who is the object that is seen in Christ and who enraptures us) effects in us (even in our unwillingness and recalcitrance, due to sin) is co-effected willingly by us through our Christian eros and, indeed, on account of the fact that the divine Spirit enthuses and inspires us to collaboration. (Balthasar 1989, 121)

The mystery of matter reveals the mysteries of the spirit. God's eros awakens our own. Worship and sacraments are thus rooted in a mutual divine/human impulse that must be called *erotic*. In sacrament, God's passionate hunger for union with all creation meets and subsumes the tumultuous human yearning for union with others.

Principle 3: Eucharistic real presence is a mystery of faith.

1.   Perhaps the clearest expression of this principle in Latin patristic theology appears in Augustine's commentaries on the gospel of John. In a sermon given to the people of Hippo (possibly on Saturday, August 9, 413), Augustine said:

> *Daturus ergo Dominus Spiritum sanctum, dixit se panem qui de caelo descendit, hortans ut credamus in eum. Credere in eum, hoc est manducare panem vivum.* (When the Lord was about to give us the Holy Spirit, he called himself "the bread which has come down from heaven," and urged us to believe in him. *To believe in him: this is to eat the living bread.*) (*Tractatus in Ioannem*, 26.1)

And in another passage of his commentary on John, Augustine argues:

> *Hoc est ergo manducare cibum non qui perit, sed qui permanet in vitam aeternam. Utquid paras dentes et ventrem? Crede, et manducasti.* (This is [what it means] to eat the food which does not perish, but which remains unto eternal life. Why, then, are you getting your teeth and stomach ready? Believe, *and you have eaten.*) (25.12)

2.   Later, in the thirteenth century, Aquinas would follow Augustine in insisting that the real presence of Christ in the eucharist can be perceived only through the working of faith. In his commentary on the *Sentences* of Peter Lombard, Aquinas explicitly cites Augustine's formula *"Crede, et manducasti"* and comments that the eating done in this sacrament is a spiritual activity, formed by faith. (*"Crede, et manducasti. Intelligendum est de manducatione spirituali, et fide formata. Ideo autem potius fidem commemorat, quia ipse est quae maxime in sacramentis operatur"* [*Comm. Sent.* 9.1.5d ex/2].)

Much later in his career, in the *Summa Theologiae*, Aquinas returned to this point. He insisted that precisely because the presence of Christ is a *substantial* presence *(per modum substantiae)*, it can be perceived only through faith. Here is the nucleus of his argument:

> [S]ubstance as such cannot be seen by the bodily eye, nor is it the object of any sense, nor can it be imagined; it is only open to the intellect. . . . Hence, properly speaking, the body of Christ . . . in this sacrament, can be reached neither by sense nor by imagination; *it is open only to the intellect,* which may be called a spiritual eye.
>
> *But it is reached by different kinds of intellect in different ways.* Now, because the way in which Christ exists in this sacrament is something that cannot be reached by the natural powers of any created mind, it lies open only before the uncreated mind of God . . . As long , however, as [someone] is still on the way to heaven, [that one] *can only know it by faith,* in the same way as other supernatural realities are known. (*Summa Theologiae,* IIIa.76.7, *corpus*)

This is actually a radical position, for it suggests that whatever kind of change may be said to happen in the eucharist (for example, the change or conversion of the substance of bread and wine into the substance of Christ's body and blood), such change can be perceived by us solely through faith. By implication, therefore, any other kind of change—perceived by the senses or by the imagination or by the natural powers of the intellect (like a "bleeding host," an image of the crucified in the host)—cannot be the change to which transubstantiation points. In other words, what happens in the eucharist has absolutely no parallel in the natural world (the world of physical and biochemical change). What happens in eucharist can thus be known, properly by "the uncreated mind of God alone"—and by us, only through faith.

3.   We are now in a position to understand why, in the Latin Catholic tradition, eucharist has been termed *mysterium fidei,* and why this phrase found its way into both the old Roman Canon and the new eucharistic prayers introduced after Vatican II. (In the old Roman Canon, the text for the consecratory formula for the cup included these words: *Hic est enim calix sanguinis mei novi et aeterni testamenti: mysterium fidei, qui pro vobis et pro multis effundetur in remissionem peccatorum.*) Thus, the eucharist is a mystery that is intelligible only by faith. This is both Aquinas's position on the eucharist and the view of a modern Thomist like Herbert McCabe:

> The change is so tremendous that it is quite imperceptible. In fact, St. Thomas says it is not a change *(mutatio)* at all, for such a change means a re-adjustment of our world—as when one thing is altered or changes into something else: this clearly makes a perceptible difference. But transubstantiation is not a change, just as creation is not a change. What the bread has become is the body of Christ, which is to say the Kingdom itself—for Christ does not inhabit the Kingdom, he, his body, his human way of communicating with other humans, is the Kingdom of God. It is by the union of his body and ours that we belong to the Kingdom. Now the Kingdom, the glorified body of Christ, is not something that could be seen within our world as part of our world; if it is to be manifest amongst us it can only be by signs, by sacramental signs: and this is just what the Eucharist is. (McCabe 1994, 220)

Principle 4: Eucharistic real presence is a precisely sacramental presence.

1.   *The classic formula.* Once again, it was Augustine who formulated this principle most explicitly in the early evolution of Latin sacramental theology. In his commentary on John's text, "The spirit gives life, the flesh profits nothing" (John 6:64), Augustine insisted

that the flesh of Christ present in the eucharist must not be confused with "meat from a butcher shop" (*Tractatus in Ioannem, 27.5*). To feed on the flesh of Christ is not to engage in an act of cannibalism. Precisely what he meant by this is even clearer in a commentary on Psalm 98, where Augustine remarked that those who first heard Jesus say, "Unless you eat my flesh you will not have eternal life in me," were stunned and scandalized:

> Their understanding of that saying was silly, their thoughts were materialistic (carnal), and hence they believed that the Lord was about to cut pieces from his flesh and give them to them . . . [But what Jesus meant was this:] Understand what I have said in a spiritual manner: not this body which you see, will you eat, and this blood which they will shed who crucify me, will you drink. What I commended was a kind of sacrament: understood spiritually it will give you life. Although that sacrament must be celebrated in a manner that is visible, it must be understood in a manner that is invisible. (See Palmer 1957, 210–11)

2. *Realism/Idealism*. Commenting on this famous Augustinian text, Paul Palmer writes that in it

> there is combined a realism or literalism that stresses the reality of Christ's flesh in the eucharist . . . along with an idealism that emphasizes the spiritual manner in which that flesh is to be eaten. Both attitudes are necessary to understand the full Catholic doctrine of the "Mystery of Faith" which is the eucharist. In the Middle Ages, realism was exaggerated by some almost to the point of cannibalism. In the Reformation period idealism resulted in the denial of the Real Presence itself. (209)

Palmer's words provide a succinct summary of the tension that has existed in Latin eucharistic theology since at least the fourth century: the tension between realism and idealism, or between literalism and symbolism. Early Christian writers like Ignatius of Antioch (c. 110) and Justin Martyr (c. 150) had spoken of eucharistic presence in strongly realistic terms: "The eucharist is the flesh of our saviour Jesus Christ, which suffered for our sins and which the Father in his loving kindness raised from the dead" (Ignatius, *Letter to the*

Smyrnaeans, cited in Palmer 1957, 196); "We have been taught [that] the food which has been made the eucharist by the prayer of his word . . . is both the flesh and blood of that Jesus who was made flesh" (Justin, *First Apology,* cited in Palmer 1957, 197).

But such realistic language created problems. After all, if Jesus is risen, then his historical body has been transformed, utterly and forever, in a manner that we can no longer grasp directly with our senses or our imaginations. Moreover, that risen body is, to use the language of medieval theology, impassible; it can no longer suffer, feel pain or shed blood. Augustine tried to deal with this tension, to maintain both realism and idealism by distinguishing between the sacramental body of Christ (in the eucharist) and the historical body of Christ, which once suffered on this earth and is now glorified in heaven.

But this solution did not resolve all ambiguities. The question of the exact relationship between Christ's eucharistic body and his historical body arose time and again during medieval controversies about the real presence, most notably in the ninth-century debate between the monks of Corbie, Paschasius Radbertus and Ratramnus, and in the eleventh-century debate between Lanfranc and Berengarius. For example, Paschasius insisted on the utter realism of Christ's presence in the eucharist. For him, there was virtually no difference between the sacramental body of the Lord and the historical body of Jesus born of the virgin. The sacramental species were simply thin veils that hid the natural flesh and blood of Christ (otherwise communicants might be revolted by what they were eating—raw flesh and blood). For this reason, too, Paschasius enthusiastically endorsed stories about "bleeding hosts" and wafers that showed a "miraculous image" of the infant Jesus. Ratramnus took an opposing view. For him, the eucharistic elements are a *sacrament* of Christ's natural historical body, but they cannot be *literally* (that is, physically) identified with that body. (For more on the eucharistic debates of the Carolingian epoch and later, see Mitchell 1982, 73–86, 137–62, and Macy 1992, 67–101.)

Similar conflicts arose in the eleventh century, when Berengarius of Tours rejected the crudely realistic views of churchmen like Paschasius and attempted to formulate an understanding of real presence based on the nature of symbolic signs. Berengarius appealed to

Augustine in proposing a distinction between *sacramentum* and *res,* between visible earthly sign and invisible divine reality signified. The bread and wine, Berengarius argued, are sacraments that signal the spiritual, invisible reality of Christ's body and blood (the *res,* to use Augustine's term). These two, sacrament and reality, are essentially related, but their relation can be grasped by the human intellect only through the power of faith. To receive communion is to feed *spiritually* upon Christ's flesh, not to "break his bones" or "tear his flesh." What is at stake in the controversy about real presence, Berengarius felt, is the nature of a sacrament. If one holds that the change in the elements of bread and wine is natural or physical, one has, in effect, overturned the very definition of a sacrament. Moreover, if this change is physical and fleshly, then the absolute integrity of Christ's glorified humanity is threatened.

Unfortunately for Berengarius, a majority of eleventh-century churchmen did not appreciate such subtleties. At the Council of Rome in 1059, he was required to sign a creedal statement whose bluntly realistic terms insisted that the eucharistic bread and wine are not only "changed" but physically converted into Christ's flesh in such a way that it is "broken by the hands of the priest and crushed by the teeth of the faithful."

3. *Aquinas' views.* When Aquinas wrote about the real presence in the thirteenth century, he was well aware of the issue's controversial history. He was particularly aware of the famous passage in Augustine's commentary on Psalm 98, where the bishop of Hippo insisted upon a spiritual, sacramental understanding of feeding on Christ's flesh. Because some theologians had taken Augustine's words to mean that the *reality* of Christ's body is not present in the sacrament, Aquinas first sought to clarify the controverted patristic text:

> When Augustine says, "You will not be eating this body which you see," he does not intend to exclude the reality of Christ's body; *what he does rule out is that they would eat it under the same form in which they were looking at it. . . .* [Augustine did not mean that] the body of Christ is in this sacrament only as a "mystical symbol." Rather, he meant that Christ's body is there

spiritually, that is, invisibly and by the power of the Spirit. (*Summa Theologiae,* IIIa.75.1, *ad primum*)

This leads Aquinas to the conclusion that the body of Christ is present in the eucharist not in the usual, natural, visible, local ways bodies are normally present, but rather in a spiritual, non-visible, substantial and sacramental manner. (See *Summa Theologiae,* IIIa.75.1, *ad quartum*; IIIa.76.2, *corpus.*) For Aquinas, Jesus is not imprisoned, captured, contained or in any other way localized on the altar. He is not a lonely prisoner in the tabernacle. He does not grow dizzy when the sacramental species are lifted and carried in procession. Nor does the eucharist reproduce the mystery of the incarnation: It does not revivify the pre-Easter Jesus, nor does it reproduce the historical person who walked in Galilee. Nor does the real presence mean that the bread's biochemistry has been altered. The bread and wine of the eucharist are not changed into some "different kind of stuff," nor do the appearances of bread and wine become a "disguise" for this "new stuff" in order to make it palatable (McCabe 1994, 217). Rather, the bread and wine become signs revealing a new reality (the real presence of the risen Jesus among us as our food and drink).

In short, for Aquinas, the eucharistic presence is real, but not natural. Christ is present not as in his natural form but as under the sacramental species. Thus, the confession Berengarius was forced to make at the Council of Rome cannot mean that the body of Christ "in itself" is broken. It can only be broken in its *sacramental* appearance. "The fraction and the chewing with the teeth," writes Aquinas, "refer to the sacramental species, underneath which the body of Christ is really present" (*Summa Theologiae,* IIIa.77.7, *ad tertium*). Herbert McCabe makes this point well:

> When we do things to the host, such as eating it, *we are not doing anything to Christ's body. What we are doing is completing the significance of the signs.* For bread and wine are meant to be eaten and drunk, to be our food; and food, eating and drinking together is, even in our secular lives, a sign expressing friendship and unity. This is why Jesus chose it to be the sign which would tell us of the real sacramental presence of his body given for us and his blood poured out for us—the body of

Christ which is more deeply our food, our "bread and wine," than is the ordinary bread and wine with which we began. (McCabe 1994, 219, emphasis added)

It is important to remember, as well, that in Aquinas's view, faith is the bottom line in understanding real presence. As William Barden notes, Christ comes mysteriously among his people

> when any of the Christian sacraments are celebrated. . . . But that grace-radiating presence is of avail only where there is faith. . . .
>
> *Faith comes before sacrament* . . . . We are made one with [Christ] by faith and incorporated into the [assembly] of *all* those who . . . have been cleansed by that fire which is his blood. We are incorporated into the Christ who died for us and we make our own the strong cry of his blood. . . .
>
> We are made holy by his holiness made ours. We are invested with the garment of his holiness. . . .
>
> [In short], we are justified by faith and, St. Thomas will add, by the sacraments of faith. *Faith is first and indispensable.* (Note in *Summa Theologiae,* Blackfriars ed., vol. 58, 201–2, text altered)

Principle 5: Eucharistic real presence is not the same thing as transubstantiation.

The final principle to note is that the Catholic tradition of real presence should not be confused with the theological doctrine of transubstantiation. McCabe notes, "The Council of Trent did not decree that Catholics should believe in transubstantiation: it just calls it a most appropriate *(aptissime)* way of talking about the Eucharist . . . it sanctioned and recommended this theology" (McCabe 1994, 217). This is important because it means that belief in the real presence is not tied to—or limited by—any single theological explanation, however apt, sanctioned and recommended it may be. It is also important to note that transubstantiation (as used and understood by Aquinas) does not involve doing something to Christ's body and blood (for example, bringing him down on the altar). Nor does it mean a passing over of the bread's reality into the reality of Christ's body, with the accidents remaining an empty shell. The metaphysics of the eucharist as understood by Aquinas does involve change, but the change is unique and lies beyond both language and beyond any *natural* process of generation or decay.

We may outline Aquinas's thought on this matter in five points:

1.   First, although Aquinas used the Aristotelian language of substance and accident, matter and form, his explanation of eucharistic presence is not Aristotelian. This is the case because the sort of change Aquinas was attempting to describe simply could not happen within the framework of Aristotelian cosmology and metaphysics. McCabe summarizes this point succinctly:

> St. Thomas uses Aristotle's language, but it breaks down in speaking of the Eucharist. It does not break down because there is some more accurate language in which the whole thing can be explained. It breaks down because it is language. We are dealing here with something that transcends our concepts and can only be spoken of by stretching language to [the] breaking point: we are dealing here with mystery. (218)

In the cogent phrase of David Power, eucharistic presence is a "word that cracks," a word that transgresses the limits of linguistic intelligibility. Eucharist defies the human project that is nearest and dearest to every speaker and thinker: the project which says all reality can be comprehended through intelligible laws of history, nature, physics, biochemistry and language. Eucharist subverts every grand unified theory that seeks to explain events from the Big Bang to the eschaton because eucharistic presence cannot be explained in terms of cause and effect. Eucharistic presence is thus a presence mysteriously—dangerously—out of control. No natural or historical analog can accurately portray either the change or the presence that results from it. Eucharist is thus an event that happens beyond language and cannot be comprehended by it.

2.   The "change" that transubstantiation points to is thus not simply a change of content or meaning, but a "change" (the word must be placed in quotation marks) *that happens at the very level of signification itself.* The appearances of bread and wine (their odor, color,

textures) do not become deceptive appearances of something else (the body and blood of Christ). Rather, the appearances (or accidents) of bread and wine cease to be appearances of anything at all. Instead, they become symbolic signs that enact and embody (that is, make present) what they signify. The consecrated bread and wine do not simply mean something new or different (for meaning is something we control); rather, they now belong to a new language—one we did not create and cannot control.

3.   The only intelligible parallel to such a change is the act of creation itself (something the Christian Aquinas could include in his cosmology, but something Aristotle could not). Creation here does not mean creationism (a specious theory that claims to locate the bio-chemical origins of the universe in a primordial act of God). As a *theological* term, creation refers to God's presence and action beyond the structures of cause and effect. God creates not by giving things the form by which they have their existence, but *by giving the act of existence itself*.

It is change of this kind—or more precisely, *creation* of this kind—that happens in eucharistic consecration, according to Aquinas.

> The bread does not turn into the body by acquiring a new form in its matter; [rather,] the whole existence of the bread becomes the existence of the living body of Christ. The body is not made out of the bread, as ashes are made out of paper by burning it (a chemical change [based on cause and effect]). [Instead,] something has happened as profoundly different from chemical change as creation is. It is not that the bread has become a new kind of thing in this world: it now belongs to a new world. As far as this world is concerned, nothing seems to have happened, but in fact what we have is not part of this world, it is the Kingdom impinging on our history and showing itself not by appearing in the world but by signs speaking to this world. (McCabe 1994, 220)

In short, transubstantiation implies a change not at the level of appearances, nor at the level of the way things exist in this world, nor at the level of contents, nor at the level of meanings, *but in the very act of existence itself,* an act that transcends time, space, this world and history.

4.   At its most profound level, then, *transubstantiation is not a change at all*—any more than creation (understood theologically) is a change. For us, change means a readjustment of our world. *Eucharistic* presence does not readjust our world but rather transcends it. The change implied by transubstantiation and real presence happens not to Christ but precisely to bread and wine. They become *sacramental signs* through a series of transformations that literally lead us from this world to the next. Eucharistic bread and wine begin as ordinary human stuff, as elements of a religious ritual meal. But through the liturgical acts of proclamation and prayer, of word and worship, this meal begins to belong to a world "beyond our universe, beyond space and history" (McCabe 1994, 220). Appearances become signs. Signs become sacrament. And sacrament draws us into a world already and always possessed by God's presence, by God's self-bestowal, by God's self-communicating incarnation in the life, death and risen destiny of Jesus Christ. What begins as a ceremonial act in church leads the assembly into the kingdom (for "kingdom" is the glorified body of Christ). As Herbert McCabe explains it:

> To be bread is to be nourishment, to play a part in human life.
> Bread and wine in any circumstances are potentially symbols of
> human community, of being one. . . . [I]n the eucharist this
> meaning is deepened and what was common bread becomes the
> sign, the *sacramental* sign, the *sign in God's language,* proclaim-
> ing that our human community is a community in God's life. . . .
>   Instead . . . of the body of Christ manifesting itself to us
> in his own accidents, in his glory, it is manifested to us, not in
> any accidents at all but in sacramental signs. What had been the
> appearances of bread and wine become . . . the signs in which
> Christ shows . . . his presence to us. They become *the language
> in which God speaks to us* and which we hear only in faith.
> They become the Word of God, they become Christ, that Word
> made flesh and dwelling among us. (221, emphasis added)

Summary

Transubstantiation and real presence thus affirm that the point of the eucharist is not the production of an object. Rather, eucharist launches a symbolic process in which appearances become sacramental signs, real symbols that embody (but do not imprison) what they signify. Because this symbolic process is not a natural one, it points to the existence of something *absent* from this world, something *missing* that only God's action can create, and only faith can perceive. In short, the church's celebration of a ritual meal launches a process of *becoming* eucharist, a process that is completed only when Christians recognize their own new identity as *Christ's body in the world*. That is why the epiclesis of the eucharistic prayer prays not only for a transformation of the gifts but also of the people: "Let your Spirit come upon these gifts to make them holy, so that they may become for us the body and blood of our Lord Jesus Christ"; "May all of us who share in the body and blood of Christ be brought together in unity by the Holy Spirit" (Eucharistic Prayer II). Or as Augustine expressed it in Book VII of his *Confessions,* "I am the food of grown men and women. Grow, and you shall feed upon me. You will not change me into yourself, as you change food into your flesh, but you will be changed into me" (Book VII:10, trans. John K. Ryan [New York: Doubleday Image, 1960], 171).

References to Works Cited in the Text

Balthasar, Hans Urs von. 1989. *The Glory of the Lord,* vol. 1. San Francisco: Ignatius.

McCabe, Herbert. 1994. "Eucharistic Change." *Priests & People* 8:217–21.

Macy, Gary. 1992. *The Banquet's Wisdom.* New York: Paulist Press.

Mitchell, Nathan. 1982. *Cult and Controversy: The Worship of the Eucharist outside Mass.* New York: Pueblo, 1982.

Palmer, Paul F. 1957. *Sacraments and Worship.* London: Darton, Longman and Todd.

Steiner, George. 1967. *Language and Silence.* New York: Athenaeum.

———. 1989. *Real Presences.* Chicago: University of Chicago Press.

Thomas Aquinas. 1963. *Summa Theologiae,* vol. 58. Translated by William Barden. New York: McGraw-Hill.

Eucharist in the Work of Some Contemporary European Theologians

During the 1990s, some very important new work on the theology of the eucharist began to appear in Europe. This work is not limited to representatives of the Roman Catholic tradition, such as Jean-Luc Marion and Herbert McCabe, OP; it also includes research by members of an ecumenical movement known as Radical Orthodoxy. (For a summary of the origins and purposes of this movement, see "Suspending the Material: The Turn of Radical Orthodoxy," in Milbank, Pickstock and Ward 1999, 1–20.) An especially notable contribution from this latter group is the book *After Writing: On the Liturgical Consummation of Philosophy* by the British scholar Catherine Pickstock. What follows draws the reader's attention especially to the work of Marion, McCabe and Pickstock.

"God without Being": Jean-Luc Marion's Theology Based on a "Refusal" of Metaphysics

The figure of French deconstructionist philosopher Jacques Derrida looms large in the work of both Catherine Pickstock and Jean-Luc

Marion. Both these theologians respond to Derrida's two fundamental challenges: first, that there is nothing beyond the text (there is no real set of references to which texts point and provide access); and, second, that the whole notion of gift (which figures so prominently in that exchange of gifts known as eucharist) is impossible both in concept and in practice.

1. *Subverting self.* Marion's larger theological program might be described as a critique of traditional Western metaphysics, indeed, as "a refusal of metaphysics." (See Loughlin 1996, 133.) He seeks to release theology "from [what he calls] 'the second idolatry'—that is the idolatry of inscribing 'God according to Being'" (Moss 1993, 395). How can this be done? Only, Marion argues, by resisting the solipsistic strategy of appropriation, whereby we seek to determine the significance of every "other"—including that supreme Other who is God—by describing its relation to ourselves (thereby making the self the center of the universe, the focal point of reality). In effect, appropriation erases otherness by turning all language into speech about the self. We must abandon, therefore, "the idolatry of the revolving or dazzling return to the Self. Thinking always remains idolatrous so long as it moves within an odyssean economy of appropriation; that is a homecoming to Self of the thought that has defused the otherness of the world, and, in the last instance, the otherness of God" (Moss 1993, 395).

In the West today, Marion might say, metaphysics is no longer discourse about Being (where Being is understood as an *otherness*—for example, the otherness of God, or of the world, or of other persons). Instead, it has become discourse about the self. This shift in focus and content has happened slyly and somewhat secretly but nonetheless powerfully. Metaphysics, in short, has surrendered its purchase on being and has surreptitiously become solipsism, egocentrism. Its center is a circle, and the circle is the self. That "S/self" is of course an idol—it is a god made after our own image and likeness. To deliver the circle (the self) from such a place of preeminence is precisely what Marion's larger theological program is all about. The Promethean Self must be subverted.

2. *Beyond an order of exchange.* Marion describes this effort at subversion as a radical conflict between idol and icon. The idol is "a pagan sun in the human firmament," while the icon "marks the advance of God . . . the creedal affirmation of a Kingdom without end" (Moss 1993, 395). Here is how Marion himself puts it:

> The idol always moves . . . towards its twilight, since already in its dawn the idol gathers only a foreign brilliance. The icon, which unbalances human sight in order to engulf it in infinite depth, marks such an advance of God that even in the times of the worst distress indifference cannot ruin it. (Marion 1991, 47)

For Marion, therefore, to think God *without being* "is to replace idol . . . with icon." This means that the cross (symbol of shame, suffering, degradation, but also icon of limitless love) displaces the circle (a classical image of divine being and eternity). In light of the cross, classical metaphysics is subverted, and God appears in our speech "under erasure," as "not-God." For "[i]t is only the Cross that can signify pure Gift whose name is Love. . . . [O]nly Love gives without any expectation of return" (Moss 1993, 395). Note carefully Marion's reference to Gift and to the Love that gives without any expectation of return. He is alluding, implicitly, to Derrida's arguments about the impossibility of gift. (More will be said about this point below.) Notice too, that once Marion introduces the language of gift, he has entered one of those "orders (economies) of exchange"—like money, sex, influence, power or any of a dozen other forms of human commerce—that are central to his thinking about a theology that refuses metaphysics and so is released from solipsism.

Marion is saying that only Love gives without any expectation of return, that only "Love loves without condition, simply because it loves" and for no other reason, for no ulterior motive (Marion 1991, 47). So love alone has the power to go beyond—to break the hellish circle—of an order of exchange based on *obligation,* a commerce based on calculating debts and settling accounts. *God without Being* is Marion's manifesto, his diatribe against the tyrannizing law contained in the very word "economy" (from Greek *oikos,* "household," and *nomos,* "law"). Every economy, according to Marion, is an idolatrous order of exchange—a perfect circle of getting, giving, spending, using, incurring debt, negotiating, obliging and repaying that is never complete but instead recycles itself endlessly.

Is there a way out of this impasse? Marion thinks there is, and he finds it in his exegesis of the famous parable of the prodigal in Luke's gospel. This parable, in Marion's view, deals with one thing and one thing only: *possession* (the possession of property, the disposability of goods through commerce, business, orders [economies] of exchange). Possession is key to the parable, because, as Marion reads it, the story

> tells of the annulment of the Gift—the gift of 'place, meaning and legitimacy' once shared by Father and Son alike—into a mode of dissipation lubricated by the younger son's desire. And the moral of the story is this. The parable, which speaks of the ways of the Father, displays the destiny of being when evicted from the play of donation, abandon and pardon; but it also . . . through the forgiveness of the Father, promises a restored currency of 'an entirely other exchange' . . . [an exchange quite different from] the idolatry of money. (Moss 1993, 396)

Marion makes much of the fact that this Lukan parable is the only place in the New Testament where the Greek word *ousia*—understood as "substance" or "property," but with intriguing allusions to "being," its usual philosophical meaning—is found.

3.   *Idol versus icon.* Marion thus believes that the parable of the prodigal reveals how a "God without being," a God who has escaped the trap of modern metaphysics, would behave. God is the Prodigal whose gift delivers not some*thing* (certainly not money) but *ousia* (Being/being)—being as "for + giveness," being as self-bestowal and self-emptying, being as lavish pardon and unabashed excess ("Kill the fatted calf, put a ring on his finger, prepare a party!"). God is the Prodigal who subverts the tyrannizing orders of exchange that reduce human life to a treadmill of desire, accumulation, consumption and obligation.

Earlier I mentioned Marion's contrast between idol and icon. That distinction may also be applied here. As icon, the prodigal God's gift reveals the destiny of being as "donation, abandon, self-emptying, pardon." But as idol, the gift is diverted from its true destiny.

> [T]he gift falls . . . drains into liquid money. And the being which was once inscribed in the fecundity of the land—which of course gives season [after] season—now dissipates into a lubricated debauchery. . . . And so . . . it is money that both facilitates the exchanges of the idolatrous economy, and indeed becomes the idol par excellence, for money marks the Gift with a price, an exchange value, which terminates utterly the infinite depth of giving. (Moss 1993, 396–97)

When this happens—as it has in most modern commercialized and industrialized nations—"money and the discourse of ontology amount to the same thing" (397). We then begin to equate self and other so that what came as pure gift is now accounted as our own property, our very own possession.

The conclusion of this process is of course a commodification of the gift, the totalitarian subsumption of all human life under a single rubric—the means of production and exchange. The impact of such commodification upon contemporary cultures has been aptly described by David Moss, who notes that money has become

> a system of . . . production and exchange much like language, which involves not only a particularly powerful thematic for thought, . . . for . . . "root metaphors," but also [an active participant] in all exchange, that is all thinking. . . . [W]e may or may not have thoughts about money at this or that moment, but our thinking—[our] way of accounting, adequation, and indeed even dialectic—will always participate in the language of *wares;* it will of necessity be a *monetary* discourse: economic, under the Law *(nomos),* and always in search of a home *(oikos).* (397, emphasis added)

All this means that (perhaps unintentionally but nevertheless inexorably) money and metaphysics have become inseparable; they are one and the same thing; they share an identity. Metaphysics is simply counterfeit money (or money is counterfeit metaphysics, if you will).

4. *Theology without money.* The modern theological task, then, can be restated this way: Theology must try to "subdue the [inevitable] economics of thinking by way of banishing money from the discourse of faith" (397). We have to seek another order or economy of exchange, an utterly new order that will let us speak of both gift and exchange *(O admirabile commercium!)* without falling into the tyranny of economics, of money-driven commerce, of fiscal strategizing, of the totalizing discourse of "equivalence and dissipation." Our task, David Moss remarks, involves recognizing and thinking about "the ineffable exteriority (that is, 'otherness,' not made by us) of God's love which has become for-us in Christ. Which is to say, learning the dauntingly difficult discipline of rendering unto Caesar what is Caesar's, and to God what is God's, and doing it all in the one language, one life" (397–98).

In sum, what Marion wants is a pure pre-ontological discourse for God, language that isn't contaminated by the counterfeit metaphysics of money. Theology's task today is thus to engage in a reckoning that does not count the cost. It must expose the utter poverty of the riches we believe we possess and control. These riches include (indeed, they are ritually embodied and enacted by) the gifts we bring to eucharist. For during the preparation of gifts at Sunday eucharist, "the presence of money, in this symbolically charged transition [from Word to Sacrament]," would seem to threaten the eucharistic exchange proper (bread and wine changed into Christ's body and blood) by claiming to be "*another place* [a rival place, a competitor] in this [sacramental] world where sign and referent coincide in the Word which is God" (Moss 1993, 399). We insist, therefore, that our collection of gifts and money for the poor is *totally different* from that *other* exchange whereby bread and wine become Christ's body and blood given for us.

But of course there's the rub. The fact that we think our collection of money and goods remains simply filthy lucre (albeit filthy lucre dedicated to a good purpose) is a sure sign we haven't understood how the prodigal God subverts all our orders of exchange. God prodigally transforms our *ousia* (the material goods and possessions we bring for the poor) in a much larger play of divine donation (think of the cross displacing the circle), abandon and pardon, and so makes our lowly money into the currency of an utterly new exchange, one radically different from the ordinary money-based commerce that exists among human beings. This is the reason why the theology of eucharist cannot separate *cult* from *care*. The body of Christ that is both on and at the table is committed to the poor, the needy, the have-nots. Hence the *Catechism of the Catholic Church* insists that the eucharist commits us to the poor (#1397).

Marion's Theology of Eucharistic Presence

1.   *Critique of right and left.* The metaphysics of being is, in many respects, a metaphysics of the *present*—of time understood simply (and only) as the present. This was the view that prevailed throughout most of Western philosophy from the time of Aristotle until the middle of the nineteenth century. Time—the present moment, the here and now—constitutes "the past as that which ends when the present begins, and the future as that which begins when the present ends" (Loughlin 1996, 133). Both past and future are thus defined by negative limits. Since past and future are precisely *not* the *present* they are also, implicitly, not *time*. The present moment determines both past and future. If there is any kind of presence it must, therefore, be "now," valid only to the degree that our present consciousness can measure it and make it "present" by making it present to our consciousness. This means, of course, that time has become the captive, the hostage, of consciousness—much as (in traditional metaphysics) being has become interchangeable with money, held hostage by human orders of exchange, by human commerce, by the totalizing human self. In effect, both being and time have become things, commodities, media of exchange and commerce that are ultimately controlled by human self-consciousness.

Indeed, both time and space have become commodified, with (in Marion's view) catastrophic results for our theology of eucharistic presence. Marion thus begins his sketch of eucharistic theology in *God without Being* by observing, "The Eucharist requires of whoever approaches it a radical conceptual self-critique" (Marion 1991,

163). Without conversion, in other words, eucharistic theology is impossible. We cannot do eucharistic theology unless we are willing to challenge and perhaps forfeit our most cherished conceptualizations. This is true whether our ideological predilections fall to the right or to the left of center. Both positions, Marion argues, are open to the charge of idolatry. Take, for example, traditionalists who cling to the language of transubstantiation. As popularly understood (though not as Aquinas understood it),

> substantial presence . . . fixes and freezes the person in an available, permanent, handy, and delimited *thing*. Hence the imposture of an idolatry that imagines itself to honor "God" when it heaps praises on his pathetic "canned" substitute (the reservation of the Eucharist), exhibited as an attraction (display of the Holy Sacrament), brandished like a banner (processions), and so on. (164)

Because human self-consciousness tends to grasp and affirm being by putting it somewhere, by localizing it, *being* gets confused with *space*. To be is to be *somewhere*. A substantial presence would thus inevitably be a local presence, and so God's presence in the eucharistic elements would seem to be nothing short of an imprisonment—God is trapped in space, so to speak, held hostage in places, things and objects. Of this God-made-thing, writes Marion,

> one would expect precisely nothing but *real* presence: presence reduced to the dimensions of a thing, a thing that "honor[s] by its presence" the liturgies where the community celebrates its own power . . . the collective self-satisfaction. Real presence: "God" made thing, a hostage without significance, powerful because mute. (164)

Marion follows this caricature of liturgical traditionalists with an equally unflattering caricature of progressives. Like those who cling to reified views of transubstantiation, progressives may also become eucharistic idolaters. Among liberals, Marion argues, the notion of presence has been displaced from *thing* (Christ as prisoner in the tabernacle) to *community* (Christ as prisoner of the community). The notion of a localized presence remains, but its meaning is altered.

Presence for progressives is a reality that inhabits the present consciousness of the collective self, and so Christ is made the prisoner of the celebrating assembly's consciousness (its meanings and goals, its struggles and searches, its political and social agendas).

Obviously, neither of these positions does justice to what the church, in its public worship, has traditionally believed about eucharist and about eucharistic presence. Marion suggests that we can move beyond the impasse created by extreme polarization between the conservative and progressive camps if we remember, first, that one cannot have or experience *presence* apart from *distance,* that one cannot have or experience *intimacy* apart from *boundaries.* Distance makes communion and presence possible. "Only distance," writes Marion, "in maintaining a distinct separation of terms (of persons), renders communion possible, and immediately mediates the relation[ship]" (169). Distance enables us to overcome the impasse of idolatry (Christ as prisoner of the tabernacle, Christ as prisoner of the community or its consciousness). The consecrated bread of the eucharist thus represents what Marion calls "an irreducible exteriority" within which Christ makes the sacramental gift of himself available to us without submitting to control *by* us. To put it another way, one cannot have presence without otherness (exteriority), availability without absence, or intimacy without distance.

2.   *Eucharistic time.* In this light we can begin to see how Marion understands eucharistic presence. "Eucharistic presence," he states,

> must be understood starting . . . from the present, *but the present must be understood first as a gift that is given.* One must measure the dimensions of eucharistic presence against the fullness of this gift. The principal weakness of reductionist interpretations [by conservatives or progressives] stems precisely from their exclusively anthropological . . . treatment of the Eucharist. They never . . . think presence starting from the gift that, theologically, constitutes presence in the present. (171)

In other words, time itself must be reinterpreted as *gift.* What makes presence possible in the eucharist is itself a divine gift—and not the work of human hands. Time has to be reimagined as content rather than chronology, meaning rather than measurement. In our routine, daily experience, the presence of anything requires that we be able to locate it within spatial and temporal coordinates. But eucharistic presence does not result from time as it is ordinarily understood; rather *eucharist disrupts and subverts time.* Ordinarily we think of something as present precisely because it appears here and now, in this moment. But in eucharist, time is not ordered or determined by the present. Rather, in eucharist, the present (the here and now) loses its privileged role as the fulcrum or center of gravity that determines time's duration and significance. (Recall the point raised earlier: In most Western philosophy from Aristotle to Hegel, past and future are *negatively* determined. The past is that which ends when the present begins, and the future is that which begins when the present ends. See Loughlin 1996, 133.)

By subverting the privileged role of the present, eucharist reveals that our understanding of time is badly flawed. "Time must be understood [so eucharist tells us] according to the order of the gift; it must be understood as that which is given, rather than as that which gives" (Loughlin 1996, 134). The key phrase here is "according to the order of the gift." The typical metaphysical notion of time understands the whole in terms of the present. But the "gifted" notion of time understands the present in terms of the whole. "The eucharistic present," writes Gerard Loughlin,

> is temporalized from the past as memorial, but not in the sense of remembering what is no longer, of calling to mind a nonpresence. That would be to think the past from the here and now. . . .
> In the eucharist the people do not recall to mind the death, resurrection and ascension of Christ, as if they might have forgotten this, but rather *remember before God that this event has not ceased to determine their day and future.* "The past [here Loughlin is quoting Marion 1991, 173] determines the reality of the present [not vice versa]—better, the present is understood as a today [recall the liturgical *hodie*] to which alone the memorial, as an actual pledge, gives meaning and reality." (134–35, emphasis added)

That memorial, in turn, "is the pledge of an advent completed *from the future*" (135, emphasis added).

So in eucharist, what we know as the present is actually determined by the past and by the future. Just as the present is temporalized by the past as memorial, so it is also temporalized by the future as anticipation. "The eucharist," Marion notes, "anticipates what we will be, will see, will love . . . In this way, 'sometimes the future lives in us without our knowing it' (Proust)" (Marion 1991, 174). In short, the present is never our possession. "Each day is given and gathered as was the manna in the wilderness. . . . What we may call eucharistic time—the eucharistic present as moment and gift, temporalized from the past and the future, form the memorial and the anticipated glory—is the paradigm of every present moment, of every time as gift" (Loughlin 1996, 135).

3.   *Not chronology but content.* Thus the presence we affirm in the eucharist has as much to do with the *future* as it does with either past or present. It is important to understand, however, that when Marion speaks of the eschatological future embodied in eucharist, he is not speaking about some kind of historical utopia that will some day arrive. Indeed, discussions of eucharistic presence require us to bracket out our ordinary chronological interpretations of time. Eschatological time is not chronology but content. This is why Marion loves to quote the aphorism of Marcel Proust: "Sometimes the future lives in us without our knowing it" (Marion 1991, 174). When we say that the eucharist is a "pledge of future glory" *(futurae gloriae pignus),* we are talking about time as gift, about content rather than chronology (wristwatch time). We are talking not about some future arrival of Santa with a sleigh full of goodies, but about a future that lives in us, powerfully, even when we can't directly see or name or feel it. This, indeed, is precisely how the eucharistic prayer can "make the memorial" of a past that is not past and of a future that has not yet happened! Ordinarily the past is what the dead belong to. But for Christians, the risen Christ has subverted this notion of past—for the One who was crucified refused to remain imprisoned among the dead, that is, he refused to become past.

The eucharist, therefore, is not about our taking possession of past and future—but about *their* taking possession of us in the present. Thus, as noted earlier, Marion insists: "The Eucharist anticipates

what we will be, will see, will love; . . . [it is] the figure of what we
will be . . . facing the gift that we cannot yet welcome . . . that we
cannot yet figure" (174). Sometimes the future lives in us without
our knowing it. That is what Marion means by the Greek word *epek-
tasis*. In eucharist, the reality of the present is determined by a past
and a future that are always, already arriving.

4.   *Presence as gift.* We must learn, then, to think of presence as a
present, that is, not only as something we experience here and now,
but as *gift*. Presence, writes Marion,

> must be received as the present, namely, as the gift that is gov-
> erned by the memorial and *epektasis*. Each instant of the present
> must befall us as a gift: the day, the hour, the instance, is imparted
> by charity. This applies to the present time (gift given) as to
> manna: one must gather it each day, without ever being able to
> store it up or to amass it [and so] . . . to dispense with receiving
> it as gift. The manna of time thus becomes daily for us. . . . The
> Christian names his bread "daily bread," first because he receives
> the daily itself as a bread, a food whose daily reception—as a
> gift—no reserve will spare. . . . [And so, therefore,] of time in
> the present, it can well be said that one must receive it as a pres-
> ent, in the sense of a gift. But this implies also that we should
> receive this present of the consecrated Bread as the gift, at each
> instant, of union with Christ. (175)

This view of eucharistic presence as a gift implies (as we have
seen) a redefinition of standard Western metaphysical notions of time
(where present is the pivot and fulcrum that determines past and
future). In eucharist, metaphysical time has been dispossessed; it has
been radically eschatologized. The here and now has been subsumed
by, its meaning and content determined by, the memorialized past
and the eschatological future of which the eucharist is the real and
embodied sign. "This," writes Marion, "is a temporality where the
present, always already anterior to and in anticipation of itself, is
received to the extent that the past and the future, in the name of the
Alpha and the Omega, give it" (176). This (as I will try to show more
fully below) is Marion's answer to Derrida's challenge that a gift is

impossible because every gift implies a return and every return implies restitution. (On this point, see Loughlin 1996, 125.)

5. *The icon of God's love.* Eucharistic presence may thus be thought of as love caught in the act of giving itself, giving itself as body and blood, a body and blood "offered *for you*."

> The Son took on the body of humanity only in order to play humanly the trinitarian game of love; for this reason also, he loved "to the end" (John 13:1), that is, to the Cross; in order that the irrefutable demonstration of the death and resurrection not cease to provoke us, he gives himself with insistence in a body and a blood that persist in each day that time imparts to us. (Marion 1991, 177)

The consecrated bread and wine of eucharist, then, become the ultimate icon of a love that delivers itself body and soul. It is this love that advances (from both memorialized past and anticipated future) to meet us in the paschal meal. And love does this even at the risk of being scorned. For Marion, Christ's taking of a sacramental body completes the trinitarian process—the economy of salvation—begun in the incarnation. "The sacramental body completes the oblation of the body, [an] oblation that incarnates the trinitatrian oblation— 'You wanted neither sacrifice, nor oblation, but you fashioned me a body'" (Psalm 40:7, as translated by the Septuagint and quoted in Hebrews 10:5–10; see Marion 1991, 178).

6. *A threefold presence.* The purpose of the eucharistic gift is, of course, *consumption.* "[T]his [eucharistic] bread . . . is given only in order to feed; it is made present only to permit its consumption" (178). At the same time, however, Marion wants to keep the door open for eucharistic adoration and contemplation. He notes that in ordinary eating we transform food into ourselves, but in eucharistic eating we are transformed into what we eat. This, of course, is a famous dictum of Latin theology, clearly stated in the *Confessions* of Augustine: "I am the food of full-grown folk. Grow and you will consume me—though you will not change me into you, as you do with fleshly food; rather, you will be changed into me." (Book VII, 10, 16).

We do not change Christ into ourselves, but rather we are changed into Christ and so become his body, the church (the body gathered at the table). The ultimate purpose of eucharist is not to change bread but to change people. Similarly, Christ assumes a sacramental body precisely in order to create that body which is church. So what Marion calls "the drama of trinitarian oblation" (alluded to above) reaches its conclusion not in the eucharistic body considered by itself, but in that reality for which Christ's eucharistic body is given, the church. The body *on* the table is there for the sake of the body *at* the table. "The bread and the wine must be consumed . . . so that our definitive union with the Father may be consummated in them, through communion with the ecclesiastical body of his Son" (Marion 1991, 179).

We must therefore speak of a threefold eucharistic presence or "present" that is made available to us sacramentally, in space and time. First, there is that "present" given to us as a series of past events (which, we have seen, do not belong to the past at all), the mysteries of Christ's self-emptying incarnation, passion, death and resurrection. Second, there is that "present" given to us as an eschatological future that is always, already arriving, that is always, already taking possession of our present, of our here and now. Jesus called this future God's reign or rule or realm, and suggested that it may erupt in our midst at any and every moment of life. Third, there is that "present" that is the daily gift of our days. Time itself is a gift that flows from God's delivery of a love that continues to flow out upon humanity as a result of what has happened in the mystery of Christ. All three of these are included in (but do not exhaust) the meaning of eucharistic real presence.

It is in light of all this that Marion sees a legitimate (and even necessary) role for eucharistic devotion and contemplation. As he argues from the beginning of *God without Being,* theology demands conversion, and eucharistic theology especially cannot proceed apart from a radical critique of self. The theologian's conversion, Marion asserts,

> first requires prayer. In this sense, what we understand by the term "eucharistic contemplation" . . . assumes its true meaning: summoned to distance by the eucharistic present [recall that one cannot have presence without distance; one cannot experience

intimacy without boundaries], the one who prays undertakes to let [his or her] gaze be converted in it . . . In prayer, only an "explanation" becomes possible, in other words, a struggle between human impotence to receive and the insistent humility of God to fulfil. (182)

7.   *Distance and difference.* A final point should be made about the importance Marion attaches to his notion of distance. Earlier I mentioned Marion's critique of those theologies—of the right and left—that imprison Christ either in objects or in the "community's will, attention or consciousness" (Loughlin 1996, 130). Transubstantiation, in Marion's view, is a doctrine that can help overcome such impasses. Because the eucharistic presence is not a reality we can generate or determine by our own unaided powers, we have to admit our distance from it. So, Marion argues,

> the theology of transubstantiation alone offers the possibility of distance, since it strictly separates my consciousness from him who summons it. In the distance thus arranged, the Other summons, by his absolutely concrete sacramental body [a body that we cannot "produce" or "invent"], my attention and my prayer. (Marion 1991, 177)

Transubstantiation thus has the merit of clearly marking the unbridgeable *difference* between the divine Other and ourselves. "In becoming conscious of the thing where eucharistic presence is embodied [the hallowed elements of bread and wine]," Marion insists, "the believing community does not become conscious of itself, but of another, of the Other par excellence" (168). Marion thus sees transubstantiation as a way to guarantee the "irreducible exteriority" of Christ's presence in the eucharist. This exteriority, this distance, makes intimacy possible by guaranteeing that otherness is not swallowed up by the devouring self of a community's consciousness, will and attention.

Herbert McCabe: New Language and the Gift

1. *The meaning of change.* It must be noted that Marion's goal of guaranteeing the "irreducible exteriority" of Christ's eucharistic presence could conceivably be met by theories other than transubstantiation. The distinguished Dominican theologian Herbert McCabe offers an example in his work "The Eucharist as Language." In the eucharist, McCabe observes, we commonly say that some kind of change occurs (to bread and wine, to people). But to call such change substantial is inaccurate, because (in Aristotelian terms), a substantial change is what happens when a dog dies and its carcass rots, or when my body metabolizes a pizza. Transubstantiation itself, he observes, is not in fact an Aristotelian explanation at all, because Aristotle's philosophy could not have made any sense of Christian affirmations like "God created the world" or "This bread is Christ's body." Such thoughts would have been unintelligible to Aristotle. Moreover, what happens in the eucharist is not, technically (for Aquinas), a change at all, any more than creation is a change. Hence, Aquinas writes, *"[Haec conversio] [n]ec continetur inter species motus naturalis"* (*Summa Theologiae*, IIIa.75.4, *corpus;* see McCabe 1987, 147). The transformation that happens in eucharist thus has nothing to do with any form of natural or biochemical change.

McCabe concludes, therefore, that transubstantiation (though it may be quite correct, given Aquinas's understanding of it) is in fact a dangerously misleading doctrine, since for many people the term transubstantiation refers to a kind of masked or camouflaged substantial change, as though what was formerly bread has now become, through a miraculous sleight-of-hand on God's part, a bloody hunk of human flesh that must be concealed under veils of bread and wine in order to overcome our human revulsion at the thought of eating and drinking such substances.

In point of fact, God does not produce in the eucharist a quasi-chemical change within the bread; instead, God utterly transforms *the meaning of change itself*. God causes not simply a change "in *what it is* that exists" but a change in what it *means* to exist in the first place (McCabe 1987, 150). There is, in the eucharist, a coming to be that is more fundamental than substantial change (in the way Aristotle understood it). In Aquinas's terms (though not in Aristotle's), we would have to say that the *esse* (the existence, where existence is understood over against the possibility that nothing whatever might have existed) of this piece of bread and this cup of wine have become the *esse* of Christ. "This transformation of a substance [bread] into another particular existent [Christ], as distinct from a different kind of thing (as in ordinary substantial change) would have been completely unintelligible to Aristotle," yet that is exactly how Aquinas used the notion of *esse* to explain realities like God's act of creating the world and the presence of Christ in the eucharist (McCabe 1999, 133).

2.   *The resurrection and language.* Such language—substance, accident, substantial and accidental change, *esse,* transubstantiation—is extremely difficult for people to grasp today. Indeed, it is often quite misleading. McCabe proposes, therefore, a rewriting of transubstantiation. He suggests that we speak of a *change of language* (where language is understood as an objective, embodied, socially mediated reality that constitutes a world). Language in this sense is not given by, but rather given to, the community. "The eucharistic gift is thus understood as the gift of a new language, a new society and a new body: the body of Christ. For McCabe, the risen body of Christ is present in the eucharist in the mode of language, in the signs we use. 'Our language [he writes] has become his body'" (Loughlin 1996, 131). Or the other way around, his (Christ's) language has become our body. Language "allows us to realize a social, communicated world as our habitat" (131):

> The human body extends itself into language, into social structures, into all the various and complex means of living together, communicating together . . . but all of them are rooted in the body; there is no human communication which is not fundamentally bodily communication. (McCabe 1987, 121)

We are aware, of course, that language is constantly changing, though most of the time it changes slowly. However, there are situations—social revolutions like the one that happened in Russia in 1917, for instance—where linguistic change is sudden and radical, and where the world "after the revolution" can no longer be expressed in pre-revolutionary language (Loughlin 1996, 132). That is the kind of revolution that McCabe thinks is happening in the eucharist. It isn't merely a revolution in words; it's a revolution in *worlds*.

> A new world is thus [for McCabe] a new language, a new communication; and it is this—a new world, language and communication—that are given in the eucharist. Christ comes to us as a new medium of communication. He gives us nothing other than himself and his language: body and word. (Loughlin 1996, 132)

All this is possible, McCabe argues, because of that revolution called the resurrection. On the other side of Easter, on the other side of that revolution called death and rising, Christ has become not less alive or less bodily but more alive, more bodily, than ever before. He is now more available in his bodiliness than he was when he ministered in first-century Palestine. Recall Karl Rahner's idea that body and spirit are not mutually exclusive categories; instead, the more I become spirit, the more I become—that is, actualize—my body, and the more I become body, the more I become—that is, actualize—my spirit. "The body of the risen Christ that comes to us in the eucharist comes to us from our promised future [as Jean-Luc Marion might put it]; it is post-revolutionary, *more* bodily [not less so]" (Loughlin 1996, 132, emphasis added).

As a result of Christ's resurrection, therefore, we may speak of bread and wine undergoing a revolutionary change when the Christian people celebrate eucharist. The bread and wine do not change into something else (the mistaken view many Catholics associate with transubstantiation); rather, they become *more radically* food and drink, for, as McCabe puts it, "Christ has a better right to appear as food and drink than bread and wine have" (McCabe 1987, 127).

3.   *"More truly food than food itself."* We may conclude with a quote from Gerard Loughlin, who summarizes McCabe's innovative rewriting of transubstantiation in this way:

> McCabe holds that apart from sexual union, there is no more primitive and fundamental form of bodily communication than

the sharing of food. The common meal is a symbol of unity because it is rooted in the life of the body. Food is a language in which we communicate and come together. Thus Christ is the true bread because in him we come truly together; he is more truly food than food itself.

When people gather for the eucharist, they gather for a meal that is at the same time the language of their bodily communication; and this language-meal is not their own, but comes to them from beyond the site of their gathering, from beyond and after the revolution. It is a language they can barely speak; but it is the language in which they can most truly communicate, be most bodily, most alive. McCabe . . . articulates the eucharistic change as a change of language. In the eucharist, "the language itself is transformed and becomes the medium of the future, the language itself becomes the presence, the bodily presence of Christ." [This quote is from McCabe 1987, 128.] This account is transubstantial because, while the "accidents" of pre-revolutionary language remain, its "substance" is post-revolutionary. The signs are the same, but their signifieds have changed; they are barely comprehensible. (Loughlin 1996, 132–33)

One final point is in order here. In her essay entitled "The Sacred Polis: Language as Synactic Event," Catherine Pickstock rewrites transubstantiation in a manner similar to McCabe's. Pickstock notes that God's *deeds* are identical with God's *words; word* and *fulfillment* are simultaneous. So God's speech is indivisible from God's will. Moreover, "God's voice moves eventfully through the world independent of our ratification. He is atemporal and acontextual, not social but 'natural'" (Pickstock 1994, 377). "The doctrine of transubstantiation," Pickstock concludes,

enables us to see Christ's words at the Last Supper as simultaneously analytic and synthetic. The statement, "This is my body . . . ," is on one hand definitive, and on the other, transformatory. The words dislocate the natural laws connecting substances and their accidents. With these few words, the substance perishes while its accidents (color, shape, and flavor) survive the annihilation of their former identities. These words transform the inanimate into the animate, the dead into the beautifying. But even saying that these words are simultaneously analytic and synthetic betrays the stuttering of human speech, for in God's terms they are not synthetic at all. For God, *these four words merely disclose what the bread always was, atemporally and acontextually.* He [God] can construct a state merely by declaring it to exist. His language, then, is the optimum fiat. (377, emphasis added)

There are parallels between Pickstock's reading of transubstantiation and Herbert McCabe's—perhaps because both are working within a framework of realist (Thomist) philosophy in which the relation between signs and things signified is a real one. This real relation provides the reason why a revolution in language (as McCabe suggests happens in transubstantiation) is a real and objective revolution—not merely a subjective or psychological event created by human speakers. And so, when Christ revolutionized language by calling bread his body and wine his blood, both speech and the nature of change were themselves changed, for Christ has more right to be called food and drink than bread and wine do. As a result, McCabe suggests that the best parallel to transubstantiation can be found in the doctrine of creation rather than in philosophical speculation about substantial change (which is open to serious misinterpretation). Creation does not change this stuff into that stuff; rather, in creation what was not comes to be—a revolution happens at the level of being itself. A similar revolution happens in transubstantiation. As McCabe argues, our language becomes Christ's body—or better, perhaps, Christ's body becomes, that is, subverts and displaces, our language. The language that is Christ's bodily presence in the consecrated bread and wine has more right to be called both word and body than our own speech and bodies do.

4.   *The possible gift.* All these "transcriptions" of transubstantiation (by Marion, McCabe and Pickstock) represent attempts to overcome Derrida's objections about "the impossible logic of the gift" by appealing to a theme found centuries earlier in Aquinas (especially in his discussion about "Gift" as a proper personal name for the Holy Spirit). Briefly stated, that theme is as follows: God's gift can never be reduced simply to the status of an external object or thing, for God's gift is always, ultimately, God's own self-bestowal. God's gift is the divine self as verb, as donation, as giving and being given.

Giver and gift are one. In a profound sense, God's giving never leaves God's hands; God's gift is always a making-present of the Giver. What God gives is always nothing less than the divine self; gift is always radical self-bestowal, radical self-communication.

"To be gift" thus fits each person of the Trinity (though to say this is to describe a more mobile theology of trinitarian relations than Aquinas would have been prepared to assert). (See Loughlin 1996, 137.) In Christ, too, giver and gift are one. Furthermore, in Christ's giving we are given to one another also, insofar as we are incorporated into the body of Christ. In Christ, therefore, gift, giver and recipients are one, and in Christ, too, we are drawn into the pattern of relations that constitute trinitarian life, a life that consists entirely of *donation,* of giving and receiving in which there is neither return nor restitution nor contractual obligation. "[T]he unity of the body of Christ," writes Gerard Loughlin, "is the unity of giver, gift and given—of teller, story and listener; of playwright, play and player; of host, meal and guest—and the unity of the Body is the presence given in the present of the eucharist" (137).

In this way Derrida's argument that gift is impossible may be overcome.

> All the terms of [God's] gift-donor, donation and donee—are collapsed into the one event that is finally the Body of Christ. God gives only himself. When God gives, nothing passes from God to someone else [that is, nothing passes from "subject" to "subject"]; rather, God draws near. Nor is God given to someone else, for the "someone else" is the being of the gift. "It is a gift to no-one, but rather establishes creatures as themselves gifts." (137)

This does not mean that God's gift is simply an empty gesture of giving without any real content. "For always what is given must be understood from Christ, and thus from the Body of Christ. The 'Body' is the being of the gift" (137). One might say that just as Christ has more right to appear as food and drink than bread and wine do, so God has more right to be gift than any human order of exchange and return.

We come, then, to the heart of Derrida's "impossible logic of the gift." If there is to be a gift, Derrida insists, there must be an absolute forgetting, a "forgetting of forgetting" that cannot be explained merely on the basis of psychological or philosophical categories. Forgetting is thus the condition of possibility for gift, just as gift is the condition of possibility for forgetting. "Gift and forgetting are 'each in the condition of the other,' forgetting in the condition of the gift and the gift in the condition of forgetting" (127). In short, gift and forgetting are mutually constitutive; a gift can be a gift only if it is forgotten in the very moment of giving. Or to put it in positive terms, one might say that if a gift is to be possible, it must paradoxically combine complete gratuity and spontaneity with a complete and absolute *return*.

This is exactly what God is and does (for in God, being cannot be separated from doing). God gives to no one because there is quite literally no one to give to, because all beings are in fact held in existence by the God who always creates *ex nihilo* and not out of any pre-existent matter or being. In Herbert McCabe's terms, what God gives isn't stuff, or even life, it is *esse,* that is, existence itself, as over against the possibility that nothing whatever might have existed. If there is no to in God's giving, then there can be no taint of exchange, no cycle of return, restitution and obligation. All is gift, pure gift, and those who receive are themselves *gifts* before they are receivers! "[W]hat is given absolutely is an absolute return, for return to God is the being and beat of the human heart. We are made for God. And this is our possibility as free creatures—who are always already forgetting our giftedness—because of Jesus Christ, who is the perfect return of God's gift" (137).

And so, paradoxically, Derrida's condition of absolute forgetting is fulfilled. Ultimately, our return to God is really God's return of self to self (an intra-trinitarian event into which we are spliced by faith, grace and baptism).

> The gift of return is given in the death of Christ on the cross—
> "a man making an infinite and complete return to God"—
> which as sinners we refuse, but as members of the Body, accept.
> It is this gift we receive in the eucharist; for which there can be

no return other than to return to the God by whom and for whom we are given absolutely. (138)

The Work of Catherine Pickstock

A good place to begin to understand Catherine Pickstock's work is her "A Short Essay on the Reform of the Liturgy," published in *New Blackfriars* in 1997. This essay was by no means the earliest of her publications, but it offers a convenient synopsis of her thinking about liturgy generally, about medieval liturgy particularly, and about the reform of the liturgy in the twentieth century.

1.   *Pickstock's basic critique.* Pickstock begins with the assertion that "the liturgy of the Middle Ages, *unlike the liturgy of today,* was embedded in a culture which was ritual in character" (Pickstock 1997, 56, emphasis added). *In illis diebus,* she argues, life was itself a liturgical category, the eucharistic gifts were not disconnected from the produce of everyday life, and communities saw their existence as "flowing from eternity through the sacraments" (56). Organizations like the medieval guilds served to sacralize the world of commerce, for they ensured that "production was perpetually crossed out by being offered in worship" (56). There was, in short, no cultural disconnect between life and liturgy; together, they formed a kind of seamless garment. The later alienation of workers from both products and the means of production was unknown.

Here we meet one of Pickstock's insistent themes: that medieval culture was innately *ritual* in character (and that, by implication, modern culture is not). Against this, however, one might argue that Western cultures today are as rife with ritual as any medieval society was, although the rituals and their performers are obviously different. The difference is that rituals today often have no necessary or confessional relation to church or formal religion. Many of them arise, instead, within family or civic life—that is, within social structures that may no longer recognize any essential allegiance to a "sacred canopy of Christendom" that would oblige participants to adhere to a defined set of religious beliefs and behaviors, assumptions, meanings and values. One may wonder further if Pickstock's vision of medieval life isn't a bit too euphoric and romanticized—fictionalized along the lines of Ellis Peters's Brother Cadfael mysteries.

Moreover, Pickstock seems to view medieval life from the purview of the privileged. It is by no means clear that medieval serfs and peasants would have shared her conviction that the world of commerce was sacralized, and that workers felt no alienation from their products. Poverty, disease, violence and brutality are not, after all, inventions of the twentieth century, or of modernity, or of Western society after the Enlightenment. The price Pickstock pays for her assertion that medieval liturgy was "embedded in a culture which was ritual in character" is high, real and human, and such a sanitized history of the Middle Ages would seem quite indefensible to many modern historians.

2.   *Liturgy as a cultural phenomenon.* Still, Pickstock is surely correct to insist that liturgy is always a cultural phenomenon. There are no abstractly pure, uninculturated liturgies. Because the link between life and liturgy is reciprocal, one cannot approach liturgical reform as though worship were merely textual or even contextual. For liturgy is always—and obviously—"a cultural and ethical phenomenon," an artifact (56). This, in Pickstock's view, was the central failure of the Second Vatican Council's liturgical program. Because it neglected to view liturgy as a cultural and ethical system, it "failed to challenge those structures of the modern secular world which are wholly inimical to liturgical purpose: those structures . . . which perpetuate a separation of everyday life from liturgical enactment" (56). The result was, ironically, a conservatism far more pervasive and sinister than the conservative nostalgia of those who (in the 1960s or today) resisted the conciliar reforms. This is why, Pickstock complains, the revisions proposed during and after Vatican II were simply *"not radical enough"* (56–57). "A successful liturgical revision," she writes, "would have to involve a revolutionary re-invention of language and practice which would challenge the structures of our modern world, and only thereby restore real language and action as liturgy" (57).

3. *Flawed historiography.* Chief among the conciliar errors was the notion, based on a flawed historiography, that the development of the medieval Roman rite represented a debasement, a corruption of some (imaginary) pristine or original liturgy. And chief among the historians who promoted this view, in Pickstock's opinion, was Jesuit Josef Andreas Jungmann. Pickstock accuses Jungmann (as well as other historians of the preconciliar period like Benedictine Cyprian Vagaggini) of overstating the case against the medieval Roman liturgy. Their complaints about the Roman canon in its medieval form—with its frequent interruptions, its rhetorical accretions, its ceaseless recommencements, its politicized court ceremonial—are based, Pickstock believes, on a fundamental misunderstanding of how worshipers in fact approach God (57–58). (For a rather different assessment of the importance of Jungmann's scholarship for the liturgical reforms of the twentieth century, see the essays in Pierce and Downey 1999.)

4. *A concession.* Still, Pickstock concedes that "most of [the historical] case against later medieval and early modern liturgical practice and theology" cannot be denied. In addition to the centralization of clerical power and the pitting of priest against laity, Pickstock is distressed by what she calls

> the gradual loss of the ancient three-fold understanding of the theological "body," documented in de Lubac's book *Corpus Mysticum.* This simplification of the ancient co-mingling of the historical body of Jesus, the sacramental body, and the ecclesial body, so crucial for the understanding of transubstantiation as *an ecclesial event,* was immediately responsible for the rise of two equally culpable readings of that doctrine, as either an extrinsicist "miracle" performed solely by the Celebrant, or as an empty symbol. Both interpretations gave rise to a literalist concern with what the Eucharist "is," as an isolated phenomenon, and a tendency to think of that Sacrament in terms of demonstrable presence and verification. (Pickstock 1997, 58)

In spite of this concession, however, Pickstock maintains her judgment that the aberrations that reformers at Vatican II attributed to the Middle Ages arose at a later period (the late medieval and early modern eras).

5. *The role of repetition in ritual.* Having stated her objections to the historiography of scholars like Jungmann, Pickstock proceeds to a more specific analysis of their criticisms. Take, for example, the charge (explicitly named in *Sacrosanctum concilium*) that the medieval Roman rite was encumbered by many useless (Pickstock uses "uneconomic") repetitions and recommencements. The evidence adduced to support this charge is familiar: repeated phrases, structural re-beginnings (like the reiterated requests for purification sprinkled throughout the rite as reformed after Trent), and the somewhat "to and fro" language of offering (oblation) found in both the old offertory rite (now called the preparation of the gifts) and the old Roman Canon. All these, the pioneers of liturgical reform at the Council argued, are examples of liturgical decline or debasement and so are departures from the ways things were in the so-called Golden Age, a fall from pristine liturgical grace.

To this, Pickstock replies, rather unassailably, that repeated verbal tropes may simply reflect the *oral* provenance of the rite. "In this context," she observes, ritual repetitions and recommencements

> appear as definitive elements of a fluid structure typical of speech rather than a compartmentalized and formalized structure characteristic of writing. In a similar fashion one could account for the repeated requests for purification as signs of an underlying *apophaticism* which betokens our constitutive distance from God, rather than our sinfulness or humiliation. According to such a perspective, the haphazard structure of the rite can be seen as predicated upon the need for a constant rebeginning of liturgy because the true eschatological liturgy is in time endlessly postponed. (59)

All this ritual stop-and-go, this dizzying sense of having arrived and then having to start all over again, embodies and enacts the very condition worshipers are trying to achieve. As Pickstock astutely notes, the eucharistic rite is laced with repeated dialogues—for example, *Dominus vobiscum/et cum spiritu tuo*—that would seem to suggest a successful attainment of purification. But as soon as we arrive as this state of purity, sufficient to bless one another in this way, we must again repeat our request for purification . . . The purity of [the] place towards which we travel, this Holy of Holies, is so extremely, and so transcendently and contagiously pure, that our very journeying *towards* it becomes continuous with an *act* of purification. (59)

The liturgy's logic is, then, neither linear nor causal (in the way that effects inexorably follow causes); rather, its logic is apophatic. As Pickstock herself puts it, the liturgy's destination is not clear and distinct but inherently ambiguous:

[T]here is an ambiguity about this liturgical destination which underlines the apophatic reasoning behind these re-beginnings . . . [for] in order to pray for purification sufficient to enter the sanctuary—which is the only place where prayer can be offered felicitously—we must already be within that inner sanctuary in a state of impossible purity. [The prayer *"Aufer a nobis, Domine, iniquitates nostras: ut ad Sancta sanctorum puris mereamur mentibus introire"*] . . . therefore, can be read as a prayer that we might be able to pray, and the liturgy as a whole can be read not as a simple unilinear journey from A to B, but as an expectant work, the hope that there might be a liturgy. (59–60)

Thus, paradoxically, in order to make the journey toward the liturgical destination (the Holy of Holies, the privileged place of God's dwelling, presence and availability), we must seek a purity that is impossible (and yet is always, already given), and we must struggle (through repetitious starts, stops, backslidings and recommencements) toward a place where we've already arrived! We can do this only in the company of a cloud of witnesses and helpers *(per merita Sanctorum tuorum)* whose virtue and merit are contagious. Seen in this light, even the liturgy's triumphant moments—the Gloria, for example—are not unalloyed bursts of euphoria; rather, our exaltation

slips from doxology (*"Domine Deus, rex caelestis, Deus Pater omnipotens"*) to abasement (*". . . Domine Deus, Agnus Dei, Filius Patris. Qui tollis peccata mundi, miserere nobis"*). . . . This slippage reminds us of two related aspects of the nature of doxology. First, it recalls our lapsed condition, according to which, we can only *impersonate* angelic voices; and secondly, even this impersonation cannot be sustained for more than a few clauses, before we must again request renewal. (60)

More will be said about Pickstock's notion of "liturgical impersonation" a bit further on.

6.   *Doxology as dialectical.* This dialectic of doxology (a constant shifting back and forth between exuberant praise and breast-beating abasement) is, Pickstock believes, a fundamental characteristic of liturgical orders, particularly those of the Roman rite. The assembly's progress through the liturgy is not a geographical movement through space (where space is reified and commodified); rather, our progress is "stuttering and polyphonal: the space through which we travel is not purely a matter of *lateral* and uniform advance" (60). In short, worship should be construed as polyphonic (not homophonic or monodic); it embraces a medley of voices and genres. Pickstock also refers to this polyphonic characteristic as "satire," where satire is understood in its ancient meaning. In classical Latin the noun *satura* was not synonymous with irony, but rather referred to a plate of various kinds of fruit, a dish made up of many different ingredients. Applied to poetic (or liturgical) art, *satura* thus suggested a richly multiple ensemble of voices and genres.

The presence of multiple voices, multiple genres, in the Roman rite should not be seen, Pickstock insists, as a lapse into liturgical incoherence or

> into subjective discontinuity on the part of the worshiper. . . .
> One example of the ambiguity of the worshiper's identification is
> the prevalent trope throughout the Rite of impersonation which
> I have already mentioned to be at work in the opening phrase of
> the *Gloria*. Its use points to a protean ontology whereby imper-
> sonation precedes our "authentic" voice, thus decentering any
> construal of the self as autonomous or self-present, or in full
> command of his liturgical enactment. (60–61)

7. *Decentering*. The notion of decentering is important in Pickstock's theory of liturgical performance. Her conviction that the self must be stripped of its pretensions to autonomy resembles Marion's attempt to overcome the solipsism into which Western metaphysics fell, particularly after Descartes. In the liturgy, the worshiper's voice is decidedly not a single, coherent, confident *persona* that speaks with sublime indifference to danger. Indeed, the satiric structure of the Roman Rite *prevents* such self-importance, such self-confidence. The liturgy's rapid shifting and tumbling from voice to voice and from genre to genre—narrative, dialogue, doxology, petition, entreaty, repetition—constantly decenters the self (both the individual self and the assembly's collective identity). The result, for worshipers, is not sublime self-confidence but radical uncertainty, expressed by frequent lapses into "vocal crisis." ("Why have you rejected me? Why do I wander about, sad, while my enemy afflicts me? Redeem me!")

Decentering may thus be understood as a device that encourages the worshiper's concentration through the technique of defamiliarization. For when a text or territory is suddenly defamiliarized, it forces one to pay closer attention, to look out for the unknown, the unexpected, the blind curve.

8. *Stammering*. The Roman rite thus perceives the worshiper's stance before God as that of a stammerer. Or to put it in a slightly different way, the preferred form of liturgical eloquence is stammering. Among Jews and Christians, stammering has a long and venerable history, especially in liturgical contexts. There is the exemplary stuttering of Moses in the presence of the Holy, as contrasted with Aaron's glib eloquence—a contrast dramatically exploited in Schönberg's unfinished opera *Moses und Aron*. There is Jeremiah's *"A, a, a, Domine Deus,"* "I do not know how to speak, I am only a child" (Jeremiah 1:6). And there is Isaiah's protest that he is "a man of unclean lips, living among a people of unclean lips." Paradoxically, the inability to speak (or to speak properly) is a condition—indeed, a cliché—for the prophet's vocation in the literature of the Hebrew Bible. (See Marks 1990, 60–80.)

Stammering lies at the heart of prophetic eloquence, and this observation can provide important clues about some of the strange linguistic habits of the Roman liturgy. One is frequently struck, after all, by the apparent formlessness and meandering of prophetic discourse, which seems, more often than not, to be a pastiche, a repetitive jumble of cries and whispers, curses and blessings, lament and jubilation—a crazy quilt without any unifying pattern or logic. Prophetic oracles are powerful precisely because they confront us with a "sheer accumulation of forbidding nonsequential abundance" (Marks 1990, 60).

Herbert Marks has noted a striking similarity between the hermeneutics of Hebrew poetic and prophetic speech and the hermeneutics championed by English poet Christopher Smart in his celebrated "revisionary psalter," the *Jubilate Agno* (which contains the famous apostrophe to his pet cat, Geoffrey). "For innumerable ciphers will amount to something," Smart writes, "[T]he mind of man cannot bear a tedious accumulation of nothings without effect."

Marks sees a connection between Chrisopher Smart's "innumerable ciphers that amount to something" and Immanuel Kant's notion of the sublime. As Richard Klein has observed, "Kant calls 'sublime' that aesthetic satisfaction which includes as one of its moments a negative experience, a shock, a blockage, an intimation of mortality" (Klein 1993, xi). The category of the sublime thus combines both subjective response and objective reality. Our reaction to limitless excess, to boundlessness, is not joy but terror.

> [T]he aesthetic pleasure we take in the experience of boundlessness is not positive but negative, says Kant. The imagination suffers a shock in the presence of infinite perspectives that, in a first moment, is painful. But that negativity is the very condition of sublimity. . . .
>
> [T]he first moment of the encounter with what we call the sublimely beautiful, the feeling of awe or respect involving fear, is an experience of blockage: We discover in that fearful moment the limits of our capacity to imagine an infinite abyss—the harsh experience of recognizing the limitation of our faculty to represent in finite images the encounter with a magnitude that seems to be infinite. (63)

Therefore, "[w]e call an object sublime . . . if the attempt to represent it determines the mind to regard its inability to grasp wholly the object as a symbol of the mind's relation to a transcendent order" (Marks 1990, 61, quoting Thomas Weiskel). On the surface, this seems simply to a case of *subjective* failure: of the self's inability to grasp completely the many objects presented to cognition; of the mind's collapse in the face of "infinite magnitude" or "innumerable ciphers." But something more is going on. Marks writes:

> The indefinite plural or unassimilable excess that defeats the ordinary understanding becomes the occasion of a reactive identification which depends on the negative relation of unattainability. . . . [In other words] "The *absence* of a *signified* itself assumes the status of a *signifier*, disposing us to feel that behind this newly significant absence lurks a newly discovered presence." Daunted initially by a repetition that defies assimilation, the mind posits the same potential infinity within itself, thereby both capitulating to repetition and defending against its ostensive form. (Marks 1990, 61, again citing Weiskel)

"The absence of a signified itself assumes the status of a signifier, disposing us to feel that behind this newly significant absence lurks a newly discovered presence." That sentence deftly summarizes the significance of repetitious stammering, whether the stammerer is a biblical prophet, or a poet like Christopher Smart with his innumerable ciphers, or a Christian participating in the liturgy. In every case, the stammer is a joyful recognition of *defeat*: of cognition's collapse in the face of unassimilable excess; of the protean self's erasure by the sublime; of an *absence* behind which lurks a powerful *presence*. On one hand, the stammer is a block that *the stammerer himself or herself initiates,* a protective (or defensive) reaction against indefinite, unassimilable magnitude (Kant's sublime or Smart's innumerable ciphers). On the other hand, the stammer in an ecstatic cry of *union between* this stammerer and that boundless magnitude. These complex dynamics—defeat and ecstasy, erasure and union—are, as Herbert Marks says, "captured most subtly in the stammering of the bride in the *Cantico espiritual* of St. John of the Cross":

Y *todos cuantos vagan,*
De ti me van mil gracias refiriendo,
Y *todos más me llagan*
y déjame muriendo
Un no sé qué que quedan balbuciendo.

Figures that come and go
bring news of you indeed: what jubilant rumor!
I reel as with a blow;
sink stricken at the glimmer
of something heard ecstatic in the stammer.
(Nims 1959, 100, 101)

The bride's words capture the terrifying yet delicious sense of drowning beneath the sheer abundance of the graces that, like waves, repeatedly overwhelm her. That very repetition, in turn, the bride projects onto others, who are portrayed as stammering *(balbuciendo)*. And the whole experience is itself enacted, *performed* in the poem, by "a phonic and grammatical stammer in the verse itself *(un no sé qué que quedan')*" (Marks 1990, 64).

This ambiguous catch in the bride's voice is yet another symptom of what Pickstock calls "the impossibility of the worshiper's task . . . manifested in a kind of liturgical stammer" (Pickstock 1997, 61).

9.   *Politicized liturgy?* Ambiguity is also reflected, Pickstock contends, by the court ceremonial that became a feature of the medieval Roman rite. She argues that these ritual additions, accretions and intrusions were neither absolute nor unambiguous. "In the middle ages," she comments, "the monarchs were not absolute monarchs and were themselves included within the liturgical congregation. Because they too had to obey divine justice, any borrowing of court ceremonial by the ritual cannot be seen as an *unambiguous* manifestation of secularization or centralization" (62). In short, Pickstock believes that the medieval Latin liturgy in the West was not politicized.

But here again one may take exception to this assessment of power politics in the medieval West. Pickstock is not very specific about precisely what sort(s) of court ceremonial may have influenced the Roman rite. We know, for example, that a Byzantization of the

Roman liturgy was already well underway during Gregory the Great's tenure, and that this process resulted in a sort of celebrity rite whose focus was the pope or, in his absence, the officiating bishop or presbyter. But the influence of secular ceremonial on both early- and late-medieval Latin liturgy was not limited to Byzantine practices imported from the East. We know that Charlemagne thought of himself as a serious liturgical reformer, and that the Frankish and Germanic rituals of both court and feudal manor left indelible imprints on the historical sacramentaries of the Latin West (for example, the so-called Gelasian sacramentaries of the eighth century).

In spite of this, Pickstock argues that medieval society as a whole was decentered, that in this period there was "no absolute center of sovereignty on an immanent level" (62). She points out that ritual ambiguity was mirrored in social structure, while at the same time social structure was mirrored in ritual ambiguity. In the act of worship, she notes,

> the Celebrant's position was an ambiguous one, shifting between being on the side of the congregation to being on the side of God. He was not simply "above" the congregation, but had to request the *assistance* of the bystanders, and was subject to a permutation of identity which was . . . integral to a liturgical characterization of the worshiping self. (62)

In other words, Pickstock is convinced that the presider's role was not one of absolute dominance or power; it reflected instead the inherent ambiguity of *any* worshiper in the face of the Sublime, of "infinite, unassimilable Magnitude." And this was true not merely of presiders and worshipers, but of every social group in medieval society. Here is how Pickstock makes the point:

> According to a model in which there is only one center of sovereignty (a model which could be used to describe the absolutist political structure of the early modern and baroque periods), there can only be a connection with the transcendent at that central point, so that everything beneath that point is effectively secularized. However, according to the decentered and organic structure of medieval society, every social group was formed by worship. This is illustrated . . . most especially by the importance

of the economic guilds . . . Whilst one might at first suppose that a sacred society would have only one invested sacred center or "site," it is to the contrary clear that a Christian society has many centers because, (as manifest in the theology of the Roman Rite), the true sacred center is unplaceable and lies beyond place itself, in God. (62–63)

The focus on a single sacred center would result, Pickstock suggests, in a loss of focus—the liturgy would be focused on the *place*, the liturgical center, and not on God. Such, she insists, may have been the case from the early modern period onward, but it was not the case in the Middle Ages.

10. *Critical history.* None of this is meant to imply that Pickstock rejects anthropological or historical-critical studies of early Christian worship. She concedes, for example, that eucharistic origins should probably be sought in meal practices that were not, in the beginning, always (or only) thematized as eucharistic. But this very fact, she argues, can cut both ways. If the originating context of eucharist was an ordinary meal, then the opposite might be affirmed as well, that is, that

> every meal should only occur as a ritual feast, thus pulling everyday life towards a ritual mode just as much as vice-versa. The community which prepared and enjoyed the feast was itself only bestowed in and through the liturgical celebration. Thus, the meal could be seen as a communal activity which took place only because it was embedded in liturgical life, rather than as a liturgical form additional or subordinate to the meal, in the form of a linguistic elaboration. (63)

In other words, it isn't so much that ordinary meals illuminate the meaning of eucharist, but that eucharist illuminates the significance of every human gathering to share food and drink. Eucharist makes sense of dining, not dining of eucharist.

11. *Inadequate reform.* All that having been said, Pickstock returns to her oft-repeated point that the liturgical reform launched by and after Vatican II was not adequate to its theology:

[T]he liturgical revisers of Vatican II chose as a liturgical paradigm a text which, as being more of a treatise on liturgy than a liturgy itself, would in the end prove misleading for the program of liturgical recovery. Moreover, in rejecting the features of multiple repetition, complexity of genre, instability of the worshiping subject, and continued interruption of progress by renewed prayers of penitence, under the assumption that these were secular interpolations, they ironically perpetuate certain features of the truly secularizing modern epoch. (63)

In short, by seeking to *excise* secularist accretions from the Roman rite, the postconciliar reformers unwittingly succeeded in *secularizing* it. They imported, Pickstock charges, foreign (and secularist) notions like "argument," "linear order," "segmentation" and "discrete stages" on a liturgical structure "whose provenance and theological context is wholly oral and apophatic, set within a passionate order of language which calls in order to be calling, or in hope of further calling (and not for any instrumental purpose)" (63–64). Above all, she concludes, "the liturgical reformers of Vatican II failed to realize that one cannot simply 'return' to an earlier form, because the earlier liturgies only existed as part of a culture which was itself ritual (ecclesial-sacramental-historical) in character" (64).

Some of Pickstock's charges about the inadequacies of the liturgical reforms that followed Vatican II may in fact be true, particularly the early (and perhaps clumsy) attempts to reduce repetition or linguistic redundancy in the English translations of texts from the Latin *typica*. But she also ignores the enormous benefits that have resulted from the Council's work. Prior to Vatican II, for example, a scant 22 verses from the Hebrew Bible were read in the cycle of lectionary readings for Sunday Masses throughout the year (excluding the Easter Vigil which, of course, had been transferred to Saturday morning prior to its restoration in 1955). The postconciliar lectionary system, though perhaps imperfect, sets before the Christian people an enormously rich and varied selection of readings from both testaments and makes possible as well an ecumenical common lectionary. More basic still was the Council's restoration of the role of lay persons in the liturgy (and in its ministries).

Full, conscious and active participation is not, after all, the enemy of the sort of ritual strategies Pickstock finds in the medieval Roman rite. On the contrary, such fulsome participation subverts precisely the power-driven absolutism embodied in a celebrity-centered style of clericalized ritual that crippled late medieval, early modern and baroque versions of the Roman liturgy. While Pickstock complains that the postconciliar revisionists mistook the liturgy as "text" (writing) rather than "oral and ritual culture," her own analysis is obsessively text-centered. For that reason, she sometimes sounds like a music critic so obsessed with the composer's *score* that she forgets the players' purpose is to make *music*.

And what of the future? Pickstock admits it is probably not possible to overthrow the anti-ritualism of modernity. That being so, we should strive, she believes, to devise "a liturgy that *refuse[s]* to be enculturated in our modern habits of thought and speech" (64). What we now need in liturgy, she asserts, is not clarity, precision, neatness and familiarity, but stammering, oral spontaneity, and confusion—"the shock of a defamiliarizing language" that teaches us "to live only to worship, and to be in community only as recipients of the gift of the body of Christ" (64).

So much, then, for this sketch of Pickstock's major concerns about the Roman rite and its modern reform. A far fuller and more technically nuanced argument is presented in her important book *After Writing*. (See Pickstock 1998.) I will conclude this summary of eucharist in the work of modern European theologians by calling the reader's attention to Pickstock's interesting view of liturgical impersonation.

12. *Impersonation.* The tenor of Pickstock's thought about Christian worship can be summarized in a short phrase: to be is to *worship*. Human existence is inescapably liturgical, doxological. Still, worship is in some sense an impossible act, just as God's wisdom revealed in Christ seems divine madness. For all that, Pickstock insists, doxology is "ontologically constitutive," it is what makes our existence as human subjects possible. That is why one cannot deny or erase the personal subject even (or especially) in the impossible act of worship, "for without the liturgy, there *is* no subject, and the ultimate and holy

expression of humility is that which voices its desire to *be* a subject, which is to be one with God" (Pickstock 1998, 196). Quite simply, we become ourselves only in the act of praising God. This truth is embodied in our very speech, for language itself, as Plato knew, has a "doxological character" and is "ultimately concerned with praise of the divine" (xiii–xiv, 37).

Our contemporary information culture, Pickstock argues, resists this doxological understanding of human beings and human speech. It prefers to think of language as an instrument of manipulation and control wielded by a "detached, 'spiritualized' human self," a self that is flattened, atemporal, disembodied and literally *dis*passionate (Pickstock used the word "anerotic," lacking in *eros,* deprived of passionate drive) (xiii). We thus live in a world that fills us with millions of wishes and desires, then renders us impotent, utterly incapable of action that would deliver us the dream.

Such technologized views of self and speech are at odds with the earliest traditions of Western thought and philosophy, Pickstock argues. Vision, she notes, was central in Plato's dialogues (in the *Phaedrus,* for example) "because of its crucial role in the process of recognition of the good" (32). But such vision does not arise within an utterly autonomous, hermetically closed subject, for the Socratic gaze is nonviolent, reverential, open to receive and release. It is "a gaze which receives into itself that which offers itself to be recognized; . . . [it] is *subordinate* to that upon which it gazes, which is the good" (32). This kind of seeing does not seek to control, dominate, master or manipulate. Rather, it is *"received* (as happiness) by the lover in his act of passing it on, . . . for *eros* is, by definition, an interpersonal flow." Hence, the "erotic gaze institutes an ontologically constitutive loss of self, a redemptive return of that which one loves above all but is willing to give away: the very antithesis of capital" (33). One is reminded here of Jesus' warning that a person cannot preserve life by amassing capital (psychological or fiscal) but only by giving the self away.

Such Socratic gazing or vision—interpersonal, receiving and releasing, subordinating itself to the Good that it loves—lies at the heart of worship, which is, and ever must be, an act of radical dispossession. We come to worship needy and fallen, not brassily trumpeting our self-induced strength and purity. This is one reason why Christian worship traditionally begins with acts of repentance or purification, like the offering of incense. "The cloud of divine embodiment," Pickstock comments, "descends upon us, revesting us in a holy garment. But to be clothed with this cloud is also to be consumed: here, to live is equally to die, and without conflict between the two, because it is no longer merely to decay in time, but to leave time as resurrected and ascended" (188).

This is also the reason why liturgy is such a blatant act of impersonation. At worship we are, quite literally, traveling under an assumed identity, borrowing *another's* name and passport. Such "self-dispossessing acts of doxological impersonation . . . displace any sense of enclosed autonomy in the subject in favor of that which is impersonated" (208). We *become* what we sing, praise and celebrate. And this is not mere mimicry or ventriloquism, for

> [b]y impersonating angelic voices or the Trinitarian persons, the worshiping impersonator cannot but participate in that which he emulates, and so, to travel in another's name becomes the nomination of the traveler himself. In consequence he does not ashamedly conceal his inadequate and stammering voice by assuming divine voices, in the covert manner of ventriloquist substitution, but boldly asserts that he acts *"In nomine Patris et Filii et Spiritus Sancti."* (208)

In sum, we are metamorphosed into the object of our praise, with the result that "the hitherto quarantined realms of the earthly and transcendent" begin to overflow into one another. The partition between divine absence and presence breaks down. The hierarchically arranged boundaries between earthly and heavenly, immanent and transcendent, this worldly and otherworldly, natural and supernatural, are transgressed. Liturgy thus makes us confront the discomfiting, "insane figure of God incarnate . . . the wisdom which cannot be understood by empirical or 'logical' investigation, Christ made man, but seen by men as a madman" (Pickstock 1994, 337). We liturgical impersonators are forced to face outrageous wisdom: a God "submitted to the most lowly of human forms, the fool," a God who "brought shame to the wise" and "nullified the false fullness of 'reason.'" (337).

Conclusion

There is much to admire and ponder in works like Pickstock's *After Writing* and in Jean-Luc Marion's *God without Being*. Still, each of these authors seems slightly impatient with the burden, the rude facts, of history. Thus, for instance, to extol the medieval Latin liturgy as though it were a *norma non normata* for Christian worship ignores the fact that what was eventually codified in the twelfth and thirteenth centuries as "the Roman rite" was actually a somewhat marginal, eccentric usage—the liturgy of the papal court with all the Frankish, Gallican, Germanic and assorted north of the Alps accretions that made both texts and rubrics something quite *other* than Roman. Or again, both Pickstock and Marion focus so resolutely on Western, Latin and Eurocentric theology that the rich ritual and theological traditions linked to eucharist in the Christian East are simply ignored. For these reasons (and many others), the reader is encouraged to read Herbert McCabe's stimulating work alongside that of Marion and Pickstock. McCabe succeeds in both respecting the tradition of Thomist thought about transubstantiation and in suggesting an innovative understanding of real presence based on modern experiences of language and culture.

References to Works Cited in the Text

Klein, Richard. 1993. *Cigarettes Are Sublime.* Durham, North Carolina: Duke University Press.

Loughlin, Gerard. 1996. "Transubstantiation: Eucharist as Pure Gift." In *Christ: The Sacramental Word,* edited by David Brown and Ann Loades. London: SPCK, 123–41.

McCabe, Herbert. 1987. *God Matters.* London: Geoffrey Chapman.

———. 1999. "The Eucharist as Language." *Modern Theology* 15:131–41.

Marion, Jean-Luc. 1991. *God without Being. Hors-Texte.* Translated by Thomas A. Carlson. Chicago: University of Chicago Press.

Marks, Herbert. 1990. "On Prophetic Stammering." *The Book and the Text: The Bible and Literary Theory,* edited by Regina M. Schwartz. Oxford: Basil Blackwell, 60–80.

Milbank, John; Pickstock, Catherine; and Ward, Graham, eds. 1999. *Radical Orthodoxy.* London: Routledge.

Moss, David. 1993. "Costly Giving: On Jean-Luc Marion's Theology of Gift." *New Blackfriars* 74:393–99.

Nims, John Frederick, trans. 1959. *The Poems of St. John of the Cross.* New York/London: Grove Press/Evergreen Books, Ltd.

Pickstock, Catherine. 1994. "The Sacred Polis: Language as Synactic Event." *Literature & Theology* 8:367–83.

———. 1997. "A Short Essay on the Reform of the Liturgy." *New Blackfriars* 78:56–65.

———. 1998. *After Writing: On the Liturgical Consummation of Philosophy.* Oxford: Blackwell.

Pierce, Joanne, and Downey, Michael, eds. 1999. *Source and Summit: Commemorating Josef A. Jungmann.* Collegeville: The Liturgical Press.

Resources

Other LTP Publications by Nathan Mitchell

Postures of the Assembly during the Eucharistic Prayer. With John Leonard. Historical source material on the theological significance and evolution of the assembly's posture during the eucharistic prayer.

Eucharist as Sacrament of Initiation. Forum Essay series. Explores eucharist as a sacrament of initiation and a call to conversion.

Assembly. Edited by Nathan Mitchell, a publication of the Notre Dame Center for Pastoral Liturgy. Six issues a year. Back issues available.

Other LTP Books on Eucharist

The Communion Rite at Sunday Mass. Gabe Huck. Explores every aspect of the communion rite and shows how strong and beautiful holy communion can be at every Mass in every parish. Includes bulletin inserts and other supplementary materials.

The Dilemma of Priestless Sundays. James Dallen. The most thorough study to date of the implications of Sunday celebrations in the absence of a priest.

Dining in the Kingdom of God. Eugene LaVerdiere. A great scripture scholar explores how Luke's gospel is filled with meals and what these have to tell us about eucharist. Also by the same author, *The Breaking of the Bread.* LaVerdiere traces Luke's further development of the practice and theology of eucharist in Acts.

The Eucharistic Prayer at Sunday Mass. Richard McCarron. Examines the eucharistic prayer for practical ways to establish its rightful place at the center of the Sunday assembly.

A Eucharist Sourcebook. Compiled by J. Robert Baker and Barbara Budde. This anthology gathers poetry, prose, hymns and prayers reflecting on what eucharist means, what it means to do eucharist, and what it means to be eucharist.

From Age to Age: How Christians Have Celebrated the Eucharist. Edward Foley. Describes the celebration of eucharist through the centuries, focusing on vessels, books, music and architecture. Includes many maps and drawings.

Prayers for Sundays and Seasons. Peter Scagnelli. Three volumes (one each for the three years of the lectionary cycle) containing intercessions, collects, introductions to the Lord's Prayer and more.

Preaching about the Mass. Gabe Huck. Sample homilies on what we do when we gather on Sunday to listen, intercede, give thanks and praise, eat and drink together. A basic catechesis for the assembly.

Saving Signs, Wondrous Words. David Philippart. Probes the words and actions we use when we pray as an assembly in short homily-like essays. Topics include the altar, the door and the communion procession.

Sunday Mass Five Years from Now. Gabe Huck. A step-by-step approach for the parish staff and liturgy board to work toward a life-giving liturgy for the parish.

Wine and Bread. Photina Rech. A delightful examination of the Bible and ancient Christian and classical writers that explores the richness of the elements that become for us the body and blood of the Lord.

LTP Basics of Ministry Series

Guide for Sunday Mass. Cardinal Roger Mahony. The pastoral letter *Gather Faithfully Together* in book form. Explores the vigor of the Sunday assembly and practical ideas on how it should become a way of life in every parish. English and Spanish.

Guide for the Assembly. Cardinal Joseph Bernardin. A discussion for all parishioners of their right and duty to become a vibrant assembly at the parish Sunday eucharist. Study guide included. English and Spanish.

Other books in the *Basics of Ministry* series explore the ministries of lectors, ushers, ministers of communion and deacons. Many are available in both English and Spanish.

LTP Videos on Eucharist

History of the Mass. Conceived and written by John McKenna. The story of how the Mass has evolved since the time of the apostles through these post–Vatican II years. 40 minutes.

The Sunday Mass Video Series. Five videos that may be purchased individually or as a set. Approximately 30 minutes each.

> *The Roman Catholic Mass Today: Introduction and Overview*
>
> *We Shall Go Up with Joy: The Entrance Rite*
>
> *The Word of the Lord: The Liturgy of the Word*
>
> *Lift Up Your Hearts: The Eucharistic Prayer*
>
> *Say Amen! to What You Are: The Communion Rite*

Video Guide for Gather Faithfully Together. The vision of Cardinal Mahony's pastoral letter as celebrated in a parish. 30 minutes.

Video Guide for Ministers of Communion. Explores all dimensions, spiritual and practical, of this ministry. 26 minutes.

What Do We Do at Mass? Children share their insights about what happens during the liturgy. Ideal for other children and for adults, too. The footage is taken from *Video Guide for Gather Faithfully Together*. 19 minutes

LTP publishes many other materials about liturgical ministries, art and architecture, music, preaching and other aspects of Sunday liturgy.